JOE RILEY

Today's Cathedral

The Cathedral Church of Christ
Liverpool

Foreword by the Archbishop of York
the Most Reverend Stuart Blanch
formerly Bishop of Liverpool

LONDON
SPCK

First published 1978
SPCK
Holy Trinity Church
Marylebone Road
London NW1 4DU

Printed in Great Britain by
McCorquodale (Newton) Limited
Newton-le-Willows
Merseyside

ISBN 0 281 03683 7

This book is dedicated to the memory of
my father, and to my mother, who taught me
that the opposite to injustice is not
justice, but love.

Contents

Illustrations

Thanks are due to the photographers and organizations cited, for permission to reproduce these illustrations.

Acknowledgements

Thanks are due to the Dean of Liverpool for making the cathedral records available to the author. Thanks are also due to the *Liverpool Daily Post and Echo* for permission to quote from an article by Giles Gilbert Scott in a *Liverpool Daily Post and Echo* supplement in 1904.

Foreword

I came to Liverpool, after being a Residentiary Canon in Rochester, with understandable reservations about the role of any cathedral, ancient or modern, in the latter half of the twentieth century. I had been to the cathedral once before to preach at Evensong on a foggy November evening when from the pulpit all that could be seen in the distance through the fog was a little group of people within a pool of light. My time as Bishop of Liverpool did a lot for me, spiritually and theologically, and in that learning process through which I personally passed I owe a great deal to the cathedral, to the Dean, and to all who served with him. Clifford Martin, my predecessor in Liverpool had said, 'Every procession is an act of worship. Go to Liverpool Cathedral if you want to see how to walk to the glory of God.' I found that to be true and I learned something also about the power of a great building and evocative liturgy to change the lives of men.

The cathedral has played its part in many fields of human enterprise—ecumenism, academic theology, music, social concern, drama, and art—but in none more effectively, as I look back on my nine years, than in the field of evangelism. To enter that building is to have an experience of 'the High and Lofty One who inhabits eternity but is yet near to those who are of a humble and contrite spirit'; to share in a service was to feel oneself totally involved and warmly supported. To be in there on one's own was to become aware of the mysteries of light and shade, grief and joy, that surround and interpenetrate our mortal lives.

I find myself in support of this cathedral enterprise without reserve. I am glad Joe Riley has taken it in hand to write such a brisk and entertaining book and I hope many will read it—not just for information about Liverpool Cathedral but for a new insight into the role of architecture and liturgy in forming the minds of people and of societies. Those who have been responsible for building the cathedral and sharing in its life will have had their share of tribulation—and there is a sense in which in this year of grace 1978 they enter their Kingdom. May God reward them for their long patience and their unfailing sense of adventure.

STUART EBOR:

Intrada

This is one of the great buildings of the world. . . .
The impression of vastness, strength and height no
words can describe. . . . Suddenly, one sees that the
greatest art of architecture, that lifts one up and turns
one into a king, yet compels reverence, is the art of
enclosing space.   SIR JOHN BETJEMAN

It is finished. After three quarters of a century of almost continuous building, Liverpool has given the world its fifth largest church, at a cost of £5 million.

If the explorer, George Mallory, born in Birkenhead across the river Mersey, could claim to have tackled Mount Everest 'because it was there', then it can be claimed with equal finality and simplicity that Liverpool Cathedral was completed because it was started. For although Merseysiders have kept faith with the grandiose plans of their Victorian and Edwardian forebears, such a man-made, Everest will never be seriously considered again in this country: the cost, the ethics, and not least, the declining influence of the Church in society, would forbid it.

As it is, Liverpool now possesses the biggest church in Britain, capable of accommodating a congregation of more than 4,000 people. Ironically, the cathedral is the dominating feature of a city which can lay claim to some of the worst modern architecture; where pedestrians are obliged to use windy, impersonal 'walkways' on stilts; where a motorist can be lost more quickly than anywhere else in Europe; and where either the blitz or organized demolition has left tracts of blighted land or given way to predominantly urban muddle.

The cathedral, at least, offers a monument to physical and artistic greatness. Here is a project that has been completed with no feckless compromise, one using age-old crafts which have themselves now passed into the looking-glass of history.

Viewed from the air or from out at sea, the cathedral tower, standing nearly 500 ft above the river, is the first major landmark to attract the visitor's attention. From the tops of

1

the Clwydian Hills in Wales; across the Wirral peninsula; northwards beyond Southport; and east and south towards Cheshire and Greater Manchester, its bulk cuts the skyline like a symmetrical Hebridean sea stack. But however magnificent a cathedral may be, its aesthetic qualities are greatly aided by its site, and in this respect Liverpool is paralleled only by Durham for splendour. St James's Mount, with its ravine on the east side, and with the future hope (!) of sensitive landscaping and planning to the west, was without doubt the best possible choice of position. The topography accentuates the cathedral's linear qualities with dramatic effect.

Yet the full glory of the building lies within and the interior is best approached from the great West porch. As one enters beneath the huge Benedicite Window, the complete majesty is revealed in a single uncluttered vision: the light grey marble of the floor and the pink sandstone of the fabric blend to lead the eye forwards and upwards. Beyond the first flight of steps is a 30 ft bridge-arch which frames the vastness of the building's central space, and in the distance; up another set of steps, is the solid stone and gilded High Altar, backed by the stained glass of the Te Deum Window.

The relative simplicity of the architect Giles Gilbert Scott's design, with its breathtaking spaciousness, confirms his wish that the cathedral should be seen as 'a vast hall quarried out of a solid mass of stone, rather than a structure of separate units'. The horizontal stress is given by the lack of pillars, columns, and fixed furnishings; the vertical stress by the soaring arches, the lancet windows in the cliff-like walls of the undertower, and the pipework of the organ cases on either side of the Choir. This view is without doubt the greatest at-a-glance revelation in the history of British architecture. It demands a legion of superlatives, while at the same time a single phrase can achieve all that needs to be said. Sir John Betjeman, the Poet Laureate, has provided an unsurpassable description by defining this cathedral's unique quality as 'the art of enclosing space'.

The visitor is confronted with awe-inspiring statistics made visible reality: the highest Gothic arches ever built; the

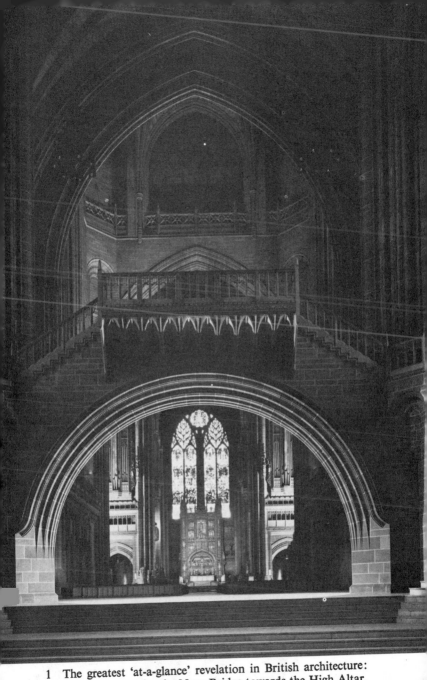

1 The greatest 'at-a-glance' revelation in British architecture: looking east under the Nave Bridge towards the High Altar.

largest tower vault in the Gothic tradition; the noblest church organ in the world; and in the tower above, the world's highest and heaviest ringing peal of bells. All this has been brought to finality in a decade when the Church of England will make over 800 churches redundant, when organized religion is on the decline, and when many committed Christians (and non-Christians) would rather see money spent on direct social needs than on consecrated bricks and mortar, no matter how inspiring the result.

The aim of this book is twofold: firstly, to tell the story of the building from its inception to its completion, and to capture something of the craftsmanship of its design. Secondly, and even more importantly, to look at the ministry and the significance of a cathedral in our time.

Liverpool is a city with two cathedrals. The Roman Catholic cathedral, which faces the Anglican one down the oft-quoted Hope Street (a great ploy for ecumenists) was consecrated at Whitsuntide, 1967. Coventry and Guildford also have cathedrals which belong wholly to the present century. But none has taken nearly so long to complete, nor been as costly or as controversial as Scott's building, spawned during the days of Empire, of intense inter-city rivalry, and of diocesan jealousies, when biggest was considered to be best. So, has Liverpool landed itself with an expensive religious dinosaur? Or, as a local folk-song asks, has the city of two cathedrals 'got one to spare'? Have our great-grandfathers left us an inheritance that owes more to pride and eccentricity than to common sense?

Building Liverpool Cathedral may have been less of a burden on the community *pro rata* than the construction of a medieval cathedral like that of Salisbury during the thirteenth century, but the position of the Church in society has also radically changed. Like the very arts which adorn Liverpool Cathedral, it has been graded as a minority interest. Now, after years of appealing to 'Finish the Cathedral', we are fully entering the era of 'Maintaining the Cathedral'. And without support and a real sense of meaning in the years ahead, even new Gothic cathedrals can start to fall down.

1

Dean Talk

> When I first came here, I began to wonder whether it
> was my job to discourage the completion of the
> cathedral. I began to wonder whether it might not be
> the prophetic and the right thing to say 'Stop'. There
> were a number of things which made me change my
> mind.
>
> EDWARD PATEY

Liverpudlians have nicknames for everything. If the neighbouring Roman Catholic cathedral goes under the vernacular
title of 'Paddy's Wigwam', owing to its cone-shape, then does
the Dean know, one wonders, that its Anglican counterpart
has been dubbed 'Patey's Pavilion'? It is a distinction which
Edward Henry Patey, third Dean of Liverpool, should be
proud of, for it proves that since his arrival in 1964 he has
certainly not been a faceless cleric within the community. On
the contrary, apart from continuing his interests as a writer
and broadcaster (journalism nearly triumphed over theology
as a career), he has been a vital force in the cathedral's ministry.

Edward Patey is a journalist's gift, because he thinks and
talks in headlines which everybody can understand. He is said
to be outspoken and controversial, only because he says what
he means: no playing his cards close to the chest, no half-
statements. He is proud of his successes and admits his
failures. When he is stumped for an answer, he tells you. He
won't play at church politics or any other sort of politics.
He doesn't seek publicity, it merely seems to seek him out.
Because he is an individual he becomes news, and after all, any
dean who says that his cathedral will outlast Liverpool and
Everton football clubs is not going to be ignored by the Press.
(By the way, which football fan was it who changed the title
on the plaque on his office door from 'The Dean' to 'Dixie
Dean'?)

At Liverpool, he followed two quite different men. The Dean and Chapter was not formed until 1931, twenty-seven years after the laying of the foundation stone. Until then, the cathedral had been in the charge of the bishopric. The Liverpool deanery is therefore less than fifty years from its genesis. First there was Frederick William Dwelly (in those days, the cathedral was nicknamed God's Dwelly House). He was the great innovator of the building's liturgical and ceremonial traditions. Then came Frederick William Dillistone, with his wide and expansive theological mission.

Edward Patey is a deep thinker, but primarily a radical doer. He, perhaps more than anyone, has made Liverpool Cathedral a multi-racial, multi-media, multi-conscious, multi-denominational laboratory. As a result, one of the thickest files on his desk is marked 'Letters of protest'. When he was installed on 16 May 1964, Liverpool was the 'capital' of the world: The Mersey Sound, Beatles *et al*, had seen to that. And within the church generally, times were changing. The year before, John Robinson, then Bishop of Woolwich, had published his book, *Honest to God*. The *Church Times* thundered: 'It is not every day that a bishop goes on record as apparently denying almost every Christian doctrine of the Church in which he holds office.' Bernard Levin in *The Pendulum Years*, a portrait of Britain in the 1960s, was even moved to make the remarkable understatement: 'It was easier to get a camel to pass through the eye of a needle than to get men, rich and poor, into the churches.'

Against this background of a new outspokenness and an apparent malaise of organized religion, Edward Patey took office. He was experienced in parish ministry, had held appointments with the British Council of Churches in adult and youth educational work, and, as Canon Residentiary in Coventry, had played an active part in pioneering and creating a new cathedral. That cathedral, however, was opened 'overnight'. Liverpool Cathedral had been building and evolving since the turn of the century, and still had a good way to go.

It was no time for mere congratulation. Action was needed

boost their morale when, goodness only knows, it needs boosting. We live in a period of unfinished projects and un-realized dreams. In Liverpool itself so many schemes have been put forward by the planning department; and then the politicians, or the economists, or both, have said no and it hasn't happened. I think that for the church and people on Merseyside—which has been a depressed area ever since the war—to be able to boast that they completed one of the great buildings of the world in spite of wars and all the problems, gives a real sense of achievement; and I think that nations and communities become great on the strength of their achieve-ments.

RILEY   Has one of the problems of continually having to justify the building been the sheer size of the project and the feeling among people that it is an overblown example of pomposity?

PATEY   People have always kicked up about the size of the place, but I think they have also been inspired by it. This is something which cuts both ways. The massiveness is in many ways out of tune with modern theological thinking. But I think that the style of Liverpool Cathedral represents the confidence that was still there when the idea of building it was mooted. It represents to some extent an imperialistic triumph translated in ecclesiastical terms.

RILEY   All very well, but what about maintaining the place? That's going to pose many problems in the years ahead.

PATEY   There are problems in precisely the same way as maintaining the ancient cathedrals. A friend of mine once said those builders thought the world would end during the twentieth century, so they built their cathedrals to last until then—which is why they're all falling down now and resulting in enormous appeals. I'm convinced that it would be wrong to envisage building anything on this scale anew, even if it were possible. I think it would be saying the wrong thing. But those who are looking after it are presented with a *fait accompli*. I'd say my job is not so much to justify the cathedral

in Liverpool to complete the building and to make it relevant and 'wanted' in the wake of mounting criticism. The first thing Edward Patey did was to organize a conference of young people; they controlled the future. He also called a wider con-ference of cathedral staff. And when he addressed the Friends and Builders Service that year, he started with the sort of talk which has continued to characterize his time as Dean: 'Interest-ing and important as cathedral buildings are, they must not be thought of as ends in themselves. They are instruments to be used. . . . Nor is it for them to reproduce unquestioningly the old cathedral pattern in a modern setting. A new cathedral is an empty shell until the builders have created life and purpose and vision within it. Pre-eminently, cathedrals must be places where great worship is offered. There must be continual experiment if cathedral worship is not to become a mere fossilization of the past, a museum piece, an antiquarian hangover. It is obvious that it is at this very point that most cathedrals are hopelessly conservative.'

The new 'headmaster' had spoken and made clear his intentions. Edward Patey is certainly not conservative. He is a social radical. Over the years his ideas have added to the sense of excitement which has been a part of the cathedral's ministry since the beginning. Now that the building is com-pleted and is no longer 'a Mona Lisa without a smile', he can talk more freely than ever about his initial impressions and about the cathedral's role and meaning. The interview repro-duced here provides the initial brushstrokes for the dual picture of physical building and ministry which this book sets out to achieve; and, hopefully, it fires the opening shots in discussing some of the main issues which have been raised over the years.

JOE RILEY   What were your feelings on arriving here? How did you view the building and the task of completion?

EDWARD PATEY   I had great faith in cathedrals as such. I had been on the staff of Coventry Cathedral for four years before it was completed and two years after its completion. There we had the opportunity of starting from scratch and asking quite basic questions. So when I came to Liverpool I already had ideas about the kind of uses the cathedral could have for worship, celebration, music, drama, happenings, and all that. I also had views about the kind of outreach a cathedral, particularly through its staff, should have in an area. But at Coventry I had become used to working in and justifying a brand-new style of architecture. I felt a curiously strange sensation here, coming into an unfinished cathedral which, architecturally, seemed rather old-fashioned. I wondered whether I could bear to come again into Gothic surroundings, when I had been so pleased at Coventry to point out that you don't have to be Gothic to be religious.

Yet fairly quickly I made discoveries. I found in the light of my experience what a very forward-looking person Dean Dwelly had been, twenty years or more before Coventry Cathedral was opened. Many of the experiments regarding community and worship and liturgy, which we were operating at Coventry, he had already pioneered. I discovered the sheer opportunity of the space here. You can move chairs about and alter the shape of the building. This has enormous potential which I don't think any other cathedral has. I'm still only on the edge of discovering how the building should be used. The sky's the limit. The cathedral has also developed a fantastic amount of good will through voluntary service. When we have a party for cathedral helpers, something like 250 people come.

About the finishing of the building. When I first came, to be absolutely honest—I didn't dare say this in public, but I don't mind saying it now—I began to wonder whether it was my job as Dean to discourage the completion of the cathedral. It appeared to be already big enough for use. We could get up to 4,000 people in, so that the West Front seemed to be, especially in the original Scott design, enormously costly—the same amount of money to build the Metropolitan Cathedral, or Coventry's. And in view of the kind of world we live in, and the economic situation, and all one's growing awareness of the inequality of wealth, I genuinely began to wonder whether it might not be prophetic to say 'Stop. We've done a marvellous job, but we oughtn't to do any more.' However, there

were a number of things which made me change my mind.

One was simply that I discovered when I came here that the cathedral had been the focus of the hopes and prayers and work and generosity of an enormous number of people, and with all their efforts fixed on finishing it. I began to see that a new dean couldn't just say to the living and the dead: 'I'm going to dash your hopes. We're not going to finish it.' I felt they could not be let down.

The second thing was that precisely because economic depressions and crises were coming, and because Liverpool is a city of many problems, and the country looked like going through a period of gloom, this seemed all the more reason why we should not be content to accept the heritage of the past in terms of York Minster and Canterbury Cathedral and just say, look what these people did for us at enormous cost. And after all, the great cathedrals were built in times of war and famine and heaven knows what, and it seemed right that this twentieth century—in many ways a century of imagination—should hand on great things for the future. There was an overriding obligation to the future to complete the building, and if we had an unfinished cathedral like Beauvais in France, then it would be a monument to twentieth-century lack of faith.

The third thing was that there were already plans for the West Window. As you move westward, the window shows the development of stained-glass art. I think there is finer stained glass here than at any time in the cathedral's history, or, indeed, since the Middle Ages. To have this window already made and stored in crates in the basement, and never put up, would have been like possessing a great musical score and never having it performed.

RILEY   Yes, but symphonies are a great deal cheaper to commission. Was finishing the cathedral justified on these arguments alone?

PATEY   I agree about the relationship of music. Before the cathedral is completed, I hope to see it used not just as a Christian Church, but the whole as to use it. It's here. Because it's here, it's much loved and much used—more than a great many cathedrals. We are kept busy all the time. If we do justify the cathedral now, we do it not so much in architectural terms as by its use.

As regards the future, we're in the same boat as other Chapters with their old cathedrals. Ours is just nearer the building of it, although the architect, in the design he has chosen, did create a remarkable number of maintenance problems. I guess that the long-term future of great buildings like this is bound to be tied up with some kind of National Trust or national finance. It could never be a diocesan matter. I should never consider it right that the building should become a charge on the diocese. As long as the right kind of *modus vivendi* could be found by which the cathedral is looked after, and yet the Church is given freedom to use it for the purposes for which it was built, then that would be all right. The difficulty is, if the state paid, what sort of say would it want about what is put into the cathedral or what alterations are made? Would it think in purely artistic terms and not necessarily in ecclesiastical or evangelical terms? You may even get the sort of situation where a charge is made and tickets are given out at the door, except for Sunday services.

RILEY   You have already mentioned your interest in experimental worship. What has been your record of success here?

PATEY   The things that have been most useful are probably the ones which have caused most fuss, in so far as they have divided people between those who thought that what was happening was right, and those who didn't. One of the most daring things was a programme for ABC Television where we had girls jiving in the central space to music by a top pop group. Generally, because we devise so many special services —like one we did for the rededication of marriage vows—we get letters from all over the world, asking for copies.

RILEY   Was there anything that was too far ahead of its time? Any blunders? And what about things you still haven't tried out?

PATEY   Nothing immediately comes to mind as being a disaster, although there are still areas I'd like to explore more, such as the use of movement. We have done a certain amount with dance groups performing within worship, but I would really like to develop movement for the whole congregation. This is difficult in a large area, with *ad hoc* congregations as distinct from parish congregations where people know each other better. I've also done a bit of experiment with drama woven into the fabric of worship, but I want to do more.

RILEY   People often say that cathedral worship is rather remote, that the choir does too much of the singing, and that the sense of intimacy is lost. What do you feel?

PATEY   This is something which continues to baffle me. One of the jobs of a cathedral is to present excellence, and excellence is important in days when people are ready to accept the second-best or shoddy. So you have your cathedral choir with its particular skills; and one reason why the choir needs to feature so strongly in worship is that otherwise we would lose them. As it is, we provide them with the minimum amount to sing to keep their loyalty. We don't sing the services every day as in some cathedrals, and so there has to be a fair amount to do at weekends. And of course people come for this and glory in it.

RILEY   You do have the facility of a mobile altar, choir-stalls, and organ console which can be used for smaller services and thus help to 'kill' the effect of remoteness. But isn't the very fact that you have to narrow the sight-lines in this way an admission that the building is far bigger than it need be?

PATEY   The building needs to be used not only for all sorts of services and events, but also for different numbers of people. We don't wish to steal people from parishes where they can have the full gamut of organizations, pastoral care, and so on. On the other hand, we have fifty or so special services a year which do fill the cathedral.

RILEY   One of these special services is to commemorate the Battle of the Atlantic, which I suppose is quite appropriate for the cathedral of the Western Approaches. But isn't there a danger of the Church being seen yet again, as all through its history, to be placing combat in a place of honour? Do you feel the cathedral sometimes becomes a parade ground or a performance gallery for these sort of services?

PATEY   This is a perpetual danger. A fellow dean of mine once talked about the 'Shinto' element or ancestor worship, and we do have too many services in this country which look back to war. But then it so happens that people who were in comradeship in the Forces often feel in a very elementary way that they want to do something religious about it. We have two alternatives: one is to say that this is really just nostalgia carried to extremes; or you can very carefully build on the pomp and circumstance and put into it some very real proclamation of the Christian gospel for now. After all, this is evangelism. This is mission. I think it is often easier to present the gospel in a lively way, not only through the sermon, but also through the conduct, sequence, and language of worship.

RILEY   Fair enough. But along with the tradition and the traditional roles, what can a new cathedral say that really is new in the life of cathedrals?

PATEY   You don't have to say anything that's new. After all, cathedrals are cathedrals, and the staffs everywhere are all contemporary. The people coming here are no different from those going to any other church. But we do have a freedom here which many cathedrals don't have.

We have a tradition that we can scrap whatever service is normally held on a Sunday and have one which is specially written for some occasion. Our Civic Service, for instance, speaks about the life of our city, the things we are grateful for, the things we are ashamed of, and the things we hope for. This means that those attending are not entering into the private world of the Church to hear the 'in talk' of the Church. They are hearing us articulate the things that people feel about the city in the 'God dimension'.

One takes the opportunity on these sort of occasions to give the prayers and the sermons a fairly cutting edge. After the Battle of the Atlantic Service one year, a man wrote to say that all he ever heard was 'Left Wing politics' when he had come to honour the dead. I wrote back to say that the best way to honour the dead was to live in a more just society than the one which caused them to be killed. If you think that's Left Wing, then okay, it's Left Wing.

RILEY   So many of these services seem to be for VIPs. Tickets are given out for seats, rows of chairs are reserved. Is this what should be happening in a 'people's cathedral'?

PATEY   I think it's the best way of being fair. If you have a great diocesan occasion with all our parishes involved, and they all send a couple of busloads, then there would be chaos. We allocate places so that everybody gets a look-in. I would prefer the minimum number of reservations for bigwigs, because I'm very anxious to avoid the kind of posh class-consciousness thing which cathedrals easily fall into.

On the other hand, we live in the kind of society in which people are put in positions of responsibility or honour. If we have a monarchy and the Lord Lieutenant comes officially, then it seems right that he should be given a special place. The Lord Mayor, too. You may say that he should sit where there's a chair available, but as long as you have the Lord Mayor system, where someone represents the dignity of a city, and you don't treat him in a special way, then you're sabotaging the whole Lord Mayor idea. If you feel that way, it's best not to have a Lord Mayor.

However, I feel most strongly about this and like to keep this sort of element down to a minimum. I'm also very glad that the cathedral is not licensed for weddings, which means that apart from those who get an archbishop's licence, the others have to be married elsewhere and then come on here. We can restrict weddings to members of our own company or to people who for some specific pastoral reason we feel should be married here. I have occasionally had requests from people claiming to be very important and whose families have done this and that for so many generations. I tell them to get married in their own parish churches. It is a sad thing when a cathedral gets a star-quality label. You're more likely to get married here if you're the daughter of a cathedral cleaner than if you're the daughter of an archbishop.

RILEY The cathedral is used for all sorts of meetings and rallies, especially the Western Rooms which are beneath the Nave. How have these fitted into the life of the cathedral?

PATEY I have tended to develop my own policy here. Everybody comes by invitation and there is no charge for use. I would say that everything that happens there is part of our ministry in reflecting the wide concern of the Church of England. We have had meetings for extreme evangelical groups; the Society of Friends; the Church of Scotland (their premises in nearby Rodney Street were declared unfit); and so on. We have also had meetings of the Society for the Protection of the Unborn Child and of social services and probation officers. A more critical area was the Campaign for Homosexual Equality. I happen to think that the Church has been responsible for many of the very cruel attitudes towards homosexuals and that we have a lot of ground to make up in sympathy and understanding. But when I allowed the first meeting, it was extraordinarily criticized and the then Bishop, Stuart Blanch, received a letter of protest and was asked to stop it taking place. However, the Bishop knew nothing about it.

RILEY Finally, what about the cathedral's wider outreach and identity with the area it serves? How can it integrate in a truly credible way?

PATEY There are a number of difficulties. One is that while the cathedral was planned to be in a nice sort of middle-class area where you might expect Anglicans to live, it is now in one which is very different. It is the great building on the edge of

Liverpool 8, one of the most difficult social areas in Britain.

By and large, the sort of things which go on in the cathedral are not those which appeal to the folk who live nearby; these, if they are going to worship at all, prefer the less formal, the less Radio Three or Four style. One of the reasons that the building could never be a parish church for this area is that it is unrepresentative of the area. Therefore, in one sense we have an anomaly, in that our regular congregation is made up of people from the wealthier suburbs who come to worship in what must appear to be a rather strange colony on the perimeter of urban decay and not a little social deprivation.

There is no clear answer to this, just as there isn't over the earlier question of money spent on the cathedral as weighed against poverty. However clever one tries to be, I shall always be left with a slight sense of conscience, even after rationalizing every possibility.

I myself have tried to identify with some of the concerns relevant to the area in which the cathedral is situated, particularly in community relations, where I have come to know leaders of various ethnic minority groups. But I have got to know them through the Community Relations Council and not by being Dean, although I imagine that gives you a bit of a handle. I at least hope that by working in this area they can recognize that behind this great façade there are people who care about the city as they do.

We have a few occasions when the cathedral becomes available for the neighbourhood, and they have a quite different atmosphere from other occasions here. When we had our International Women's Year Service, we got groups of different ethnic minority groups from the area to make statements about their hopes and fears for the role of women in their own countries, and this involved all sorts of work with groups from the area. The Jamaican Association came to celebrate the Independence Day with an informal service. We could develop this idea a great deal more. But one doesn't want to give the impression that we are forcing ourselves on people; rather, that the cathedral is an available and welcoming place.

This was how Dean Edward Patey talked about some of his feelings for the cathedral today. But to understand how the cathedral came into being and what motivated its inception, we must go back to the days of the founding of the Liverpool diocese, and earlier still.

2

Prelude and Feud

> If we mean to have a cathedral, it is our duty to begin
> work, and if we do not live to see it completed, I
> believe those who come after us will place the top
> stone upon it.
>
> JOHN CHARLES RYLE

Once upon a time there were tiny clusters of rather trouble-
some natives, mainly farmers and fishermen, who needed to
be beaten into shape, clubbed about the head, or occasionally
put to death because they resented foreigners tramping all
over their land and telling them what to do. The natives were
what are now called Liverpudlians; the foreigners were
Romans. No Merseyside County Council or Liverpool City
Council in those days: just the province of Maxima Caesari-
ensis, which had the distinction of being administered
personally by the emperors. They were prepared to leave more
settled areas in the care of the senate, whereas here, a military
force was needed for the sake of public security.

Then something quite alien to the beating and clubbing and
putting to death occurred (at least for minor offences). The
Roman Empire became Christian and in the capital of the
province, Eboracum, a bishop's headquarters were set up.
The headquarters remained until the Romans packed their
togas and went home 250 years later.

But Christianity suffered a setback; in fact, it virtually
vanished until Augustine converted King Edwin of North-
umbria in the year 627. Then the see of Eboracum was
restored and the name was corrupted by the English into
York. Next, a new bishopric was formed at Lichfield which
stayed intact until the Reformation 900 years later. Mon-
asteries had been springing up here and there, and the most
splendid in the Lichfield see was that dedicated to St Werburga
at Chester (now the cathedral). In 1541 a new see was

18

assigned to the northern half of the Lichfield diocese, including South Lancashire. Despite the wealth of the Werburga 'powerhouse', the area was still one of the poorest in England as far as ordinary people were concerned; and the people themselves were still somewhat savage, if rather less so than in the Roman era.

Less than 300 years later the Industrial Revolution entered their lives—a smoky, oily, noisy thing for which a cure has never been found. But it did mean money, and lots of it. Between them Christianity and money were as successful as the old formula of Christianity and slave labour when it came to building churches. It was taken for granted that every diocese should have a cathedral. After all, a see springs from a mother church. The Chapter and canons who counselled bishops met there, and it was also the place where a bishop had his cathedra, the seat from which he made public and formal pronouncements. Here the ritual offices were carried out in their completest and most impressive form. As time went on, the dean, as head of the Chapter, assumed a distinct role, looking after the order of worship and maintaining the fabric of the cathedral.

Liverpool had been granted a charter by King John in 1205. By 1356 the first church, dedicated to St Nicholas, had been built on the waterfront, and by 1699 a Liverpool parish had been carved out, with rectors appointed at Liverpool and Walton. By the same Act of Parliament permission was given for another church, St Peter's, to be built in the middle of the town. Increased power and wealth gave the emergent area of South Lancashire a new status. Like Topsy, Liverpool just grew. By the second half of the nineteenth century the port's sea trade was double that of London and serving half of Britain's needs. Cotton, sugar, insurance, and a host of other big commercial interests became settled here. So did nearly half a million Irish in the wake of the potato famine. There were also large settlements of Welsh and Scots, and from overseas came considerable numbers of Negroes, Chinese, and Jews. Cosmopolitan Merseyside was here to stay. The wealthy housed themselves in extensive residential suburbs with huge parks. For communal prestige they built the great William Brown Street façade of art gallery, museum, and library. Across the way they put up the finest 'modern' classical building in Europe, St George's Hall.

Liverpool was growing too big to pay lip service to the Chester diocese, of which it was part. Other cities, too, wished to flaunt their ecclesiastical independence. Nearby, a new bishopric based on Manchester was set up in 1847 to serve East and North Lancashire. Merseyside was thought to be losing religious glitter. In 1876 the crunch came: a Liverpool Bishopric Fund was launched. The idea was to raise an endowment of £100,000 to provide a bishop's salary of £3,500 a year (proportionally far greater than the present figure!). Two years later the Additional Bishoprics Act envisaged the setting up of new dioceses in Wakefield, Newcastle, and Southwell as well as Liverpool. The Merseysiders were first off the mark in raising their cash and the diocese was given the go-ahead in March 1880. It was actually formed on 19 April, the same day that Liverpool became a city. Already there were murmurings that St Peter's Church, which was to become the pro-cathedral, would be too small. Something more majestic was required, and one site, St John's Church-yard, by St George's Hall, had been mentioned by some as possible cathedral territory. Others said that St Peter's could be pulled down and a new building erected there.

But before we examine the intrigues of cathedral siting and building, it is necessary to take stock of the political tactics which led to the appointment of Liverpool's first bishop, John Charles Ryle.

To the present, the diocese has had six bishops. One of them, Stuart Blanch, left to become Archbishop of York in 1975, the first such honour for the area. The others have all made their individual mark on the work of the diocese, but none have had as great an influence on the question of the cathedral project as John Ryle, and more particularly his successor, Francis James Chavasse.

The Dean and Chapter was founded only in 1931, when Albert Augustus David was bishop. Until then, the bishops had been given direct influence over cathedral schemes and the order of worship. And it was Ryle and Chavasse who faced the overtures from those who were determined to see a cathedral built. But if Ryle had the idea somewhat thrust upon him, then that pressure was slight compared with the blunt political conniving which had installed him in the first place. The full story is told by Peter Toon and Michael Smout in their excellent book, *John Charles Ryle, Evangelical Bishop* (J. Clarke 1976). Ryle was sixty-four and had just been named as Dean of Salisbury. A native of Macclesfield, he had studied at Eton and at Christ Church, Oxford. After a life of mainly rural ministry in Suffolk, he was made honorary Dean of Norwich in 1871. (Salisbury, with its Chilmark limestone cathedral and quiet cloisters, would have been an idyllic place for this famous writer to end his days.)

All was well until Britain went to the polls in February 1880. Benjamin Disraeli was driven from power by Gladstone, but before he handed over, he made sure that John Ryle was on the train north to become Liverpool's first bishop. The Tories even provided the endowment and bought the palace in Abercromby Square, where today it forms part of the university complex (another palace was later bought at Woolton). Lord Sandon, MP for Liverpool, was heard to say that his future depended on the Protestants being kept sweet. Ryle was the no-nonsense opponent of Romanism and ritual to make that possible. Queen Victoria consented for once to be amused with the idea and Ryle was sent London-bound to be given the news by Sandon: 'We go out of office next Monday. If you don't make up your mind, we shall lose the bishopric of Liverpool.' Ryle decided virtually on the spot, and agreed to take on a new life in a bustling city. His diocese ran from Southport in the north to Widnes in the south, and east to Wigan. In his charge were 'an extraordinary variety of classes' —shipworkers, millhands, coalface workers, merchants, factory staffs, and farmers. They added up to 1,100,000 people. If politically it was game, set, and match to the Conservatives, the question of a new cathedral was still unanswered. The pressure for building came from the same group of people: the rich and the influential.

Ryle's first mention of the idea came at his consecration in York: the Minster was beautiful; Liverpool could do with a cathedral of its own. But as a good evangelical, Ryle's heart was in smaller, more intimate parish mission with 'neither a street, nor a lane, nor a house, nor a garret, nor a cellar, nor a family which is not regularly looked after'. His grass-roots approach saw twenty-seven churches and forty-eight mission halls finished by 1890. To the annoyance of the pro-cathedral brigade, some of the wealthy who would be expected to donate to such an enterprise preferred to support Ryle's ideals.

Incumbents, confirmation candidates, congregations, and Sunday school classes grew, but so did the population. It was a qualified success, despite Gladstone's understandable criticisms at Westminster, when he used a *Liverpool Daily Post* survey of attendance figures to argue against setting up a diocese of Bristol. Gladstone, who had been born in Liverpool's Rodney Street, was still feeling sore over Disraeli's coup in securing office for Ryle, so his words had a hollow ring.

Meanwhile, the cathedral-pushers were not very happy when Ryle said that his 'first and foremost business as bishop was to provide for the preaching of the gospel to souls whom no cathedral would touch'. The cost had to be set against the primary aim of 'spreading the word'. Apart from that, the whole cathedral debate bored Ryle the missionary. And he had other worries and controversies to face, like the prosecution of a cleric for 'Romanizing' a local church with ritual, and the consecrating of another church where good Anglicans thought ritual might occur.

However, a committee met in 1883 to discuss possible sites for a cathedral. The year before, some people had become over-excited at the sound of Dean Hanson, from recently divorced Chester, talking to the diocesan conference on the case for a cathedral. He was indeed a prophet from another country. From the scrum of ideas on siting, the St John's plot of land by St George's Hall won support. Discounted were St Peter's Pro-Cathedral, Monument Place, and what is now the site of the cathedral on St James's Mount. Ryle liked the choice because it was at the city centre, but was guarded in comment: 'As to the capabilities of the site for the erection of a building worthy of the second city of the Empire, I shall not trust myself to give an opinion. I will only say that it is declared to be such by one of the most experienced architects of the day. If we mean to have a cathedral, it is our duty to begin work, and if we do not live to see it completed, I believe those who come after will place the top stone upon it.'

It was competition time for a design and the winner was William Emerson, who produced a Gothic plan showing a dome not unlike Brunelleschi's Florence Cathedral. But support for the St John's site was going cold: it was said to be too near St George's Hall for it to be seen to best advantage.

By 1888 the Parliamentary vote which had allowed the setting up of a cathedral committee had become redundant, and there was a trade slump. Emerson's plans were buried and the cathedral idea was put on half-ice. An ever-so-gentlemanly feud was brewing among the high and mighty. The bishop told his diocesan conference the same year that the position of the scheme was 'rather humbling', and went on: 'I am not surprised that churchmen at a distance, who do not understand Liverpool, speak rather sceptically of us.'

More talk, more suggestions, and more lobbying followed. In 1896, Ryle spoke of 'many wearisome meetings', while Sir William Forwood, who in 1901 was to become the first chairman of the executive for the present cathedral, went on record as saying: 'The bishop did not help the cause (over the question of site), for although, in a way, he was anxious that a cathedral should be built, he freely expressed his opinion in public and private that additional churches and mission halls would be more useful.'

Ryle was more concerned over what he called 'perishing multitudes' than 'material buildings', by which, of course, he meant a cathedral of the size to accommodate the current Liverpudlian ego. The cathedral, he felt, was to 'justify the tastes of a few'. The Bishop's main monument to mission on Merseyside was to be Church House, although the original building was blitzed during the Second World War. He retired to Lowestoft in 1900 and died shortly afterwards. He now lies buried at All Saint's, Childwall and is commemorated by a recumbent effigy, designed by Giles Scott, within the cathedral he had only half wished for.

His successor, Francis Chavasse, arrived on the scene at a time of great hopes—and frustrations. After seven years of discussion, Emerson's plans had been 'laid to rest'. Apart from the siting problem, the committee had felt that an attempt to adapt Gothic architecture to a similar layout to that of St Paul's, London, would not get sufficient public support. Although in retrospect their decision was wise, its timing dashed the hopes of those who were banking on a massive demonstration of grandeur by the Liverpool diocese.

Luckily for them, Chavasse seemed more keen on the embryonic scheme than had Ryle. One of his first official acts was to revive the cathedral committee. This time attention was focused on St James's Mount: it had good elevation above the river; comparative isolation from surrounding buildings; the neighbourhood was free from noise and traffic; no diversion of streets was needed; and it was near the centre of commercial and domestic gravity. The committee ruminated and urged that it should be adopted, the Bishop supported them, and the scheme was launched at a public meeting in the town hall on 17 June 1901, with Lord Derby in the chair. Liverpool Cathedral was ready for take-off.

As Vere Cotton was to point out in his book on Liverpool Cathedral: 'With the exception of Durham, no English cathedral is so well placed to be seen at advantage both from a distance and from its immediate vicinity.'

In 1902 the Liverpool Cathedral Act continued the committee constituted earlier, said that St Nicholas's at the Pier Head should become the parish church when the first part of the cathedral was opened, and gave the go-ahead for the demolition of St Peter's. Money from the sale of site would be used to start a cathedral chapter; in the meantime the Bishop would carry out the function of Dean. St James's Mount was bought from the local authority for the astonishingly low price of £10,000. (One of the earlier sites considered would have cost £300,000!)

Chavasse had been making encouraging noises ever since he took office. In his presidential address to the Diocesan Conference in 1900, he had urged that a cathedral should do justice to the city and the Church of England. 'A poor cathedral which costs the diocese nothing in the way of self-sacrifice and which is very little superior to some of the new parish churches which have recently sprung up in Lancashire and Cheshire, would create widespread disappointment.' He went on to make a number of other points:

1   If the whole of the project could not be undertaken at once, it should be done piecemeal, as in the Middle Ages. 'If our generation can raise only £100,000, let it put up the choir or part of it, and let those who come after us complete it.'

2   It should be built by the rich and the poor and for everyone's use. 'It must be a cathedral of the people, built by them, thronged by them, loved by them; their pride, their glory, their spiritual home.' He urged that all parishes should make a contribution.

3   It should be in touch with the needs of the times. And in a purple passage, Chavasse said: 'In the cathedral of which I dream there would be daily services of the best and most reverent kind for the rich and the poor, at hours suited to both. There would be smaller chapels where quiet days for clergy and laiety would be held, and where lectures on church questions would be delivered. Attached to it would be a staff of cathedral clergy, not holding other benefices, but living and working entirely for the diocese. There would be canons to whom would be entrusted the oversight of religious education, the management of parochial missions, the supervision of junior clergy, the fostering of an interest in the spread of the gospel at home and abroad. There would be clergy able to look after vacant parishes, and to go to the help of sick vicars. There would be others with special gifts for preaching, who would assist the clergy by taking courses of sermons in Lent

and Advent, and by lecturing throughout the diocese on Christian evidences, biblical criticism, church history, and the best methods of church work. There would be something like a central school of church music, which, while seeking to make our singing more congregational than it is at present, would set the tone of a high-class and devoted service.'

4   The present church team work and social work must not be pushed into second place. 'Our schools, our poor, our hospitals, our many great institutions, our social ventures, must not be starved. The great populations of Orrell, Fazakerley, Wavertree, Mossley Hill, Skelmersdale, and Walton, which now cry out for new churches, must not be allowed to cry in vain.'

The scene was set for the building of a cathedral. Out of the mouth of the Bishop had come the right weight of words; from the maunderings of the committee, the right choice of location. Now all that was needed was an architect, a new design, and the cash to carry out the plan.

3

Great Scott

Liverpool will have a Gothic cathedral, but of a quite different type to our medieval cathedrals; in fact, there is no Gothic building in the world to which it can be compared.

GILES GILBERT SCOTT

No one can visit Liverpool Cathedral and remain indifferent to the experience: some love it; others hate it; most, at least, admire it.

On the odd day of the year when the tower is capped by mist which has drifted inland from the Mersey estuary, it looks as though Jacob has returned his ladder from the heavens. After torrential rain borne by Atlantic gales has imbued the fabric with a dark stain, the appearance is sombre and craggy. And when the sun shines, then the full relief of the masonry and every detail of the gigantic buttressing is projected outwards to the sight. The apparent indestructibility of the mass is seen to be etched and barnacled with subtle detail. Seabirds (and sometimes kestrels) circle the summit and the lesser heights, and perch with microscopic precision on the corried crevices and outer turrets of the tower.

Inside, the cathedral can be a tremendously lonely or a very rousing place. Empty, and in the half-light, the space is cavernous, almost threatening. Yet packed to the brim, filled with singing, organ music, and brass fanfares, the ethereal quality of soundwaves rebounding from stone and swirling into extinction, it is unsurpassed. The cathedral even has its own smell—the cool, minty, spicy aroma of cut rock.

Virtually all of this vision—solid and implied—is the genius of one man, the architect Giles Gilbert Scott. From the beginning of the century until his death in 1960, the vision was constantly evolving and maturing. What has resulted bears no resemblance to his original concept, nor the second. It is an on-going testament to the heroics of his imagination,

2　A great partnership: Giles Gilbert Scott (left) with the first Dean, Frederick Dwelly.

because for Scott there was no full stop which could not be turned into a comma.

Years before the first stone for the cathedral was laid, and ever since, people have either volunteered or imposed their views about its architectural and theological potential. But whereas theology can be tailored to the day, blocks of sandstone present a weightier problem: once they are in position, they don't budge with the vagaries of fashion. The choice of design, therefore, could never have been something to satisfy a transitory whim, but was fundamental to the whole future.

The dawn of the twentieth century was not really the most receptive period in history to whizz-kids. Imagine the mutterings behind many an Edwardian moustache when Scott, at twenty-two, was placed first by the assessors for his cathedral plans, knocking out the hopes of 102 other competitors from Europe and America.

In September 1901 the committee had decided that 'the

style shall be Gothic'—a view which caused considerable anger in the architectural world. An editorial in *The Builder* magazine called it 'a foolish and mischievous resolution', and a letter to *The Times* said that it invoked 'the deadly spirit of plagiarism'. The reason for the outcry was that, despite the history of Gothic architecture, its advocacy was losing ground, at least for church building. Westminster Cathedral had been started in 1895 and had broken the tradition. The *Architectural Review* argued that the stipulation was against progressive ideas, and in 1902 *The Builder* said that the assessors had not understood 'what a cathedral should be'. Many eminent men thought we were now entering an age of building railway stations, hotels, and villas rather than cathedrals. But in the end, and despite the fact that the committee was to withdraw its Gothic edict, only a small number of Renaissance and classical designs were submitted. The committee could therefore claim to have opted for their Gothic preference with full justification.

The men advising the cathedral committee were leading architects G. F. Bodley and R. Norman Shaw. They reported: 'What we had to find was not the best or the most beautiful drawings, but the best idea and the finest conception. Many of the drawings are attractive, but we had to look further than that. We had to look for the real effect of the building rising to its final completion, at the dimensions and proportions of the different parts such as the piers and arches of the great Nave; we had to look at the practical and feasible aspects of the designs; we had to look for a sufficiently original conception; we had to look for a fine and noble proportion combined with an evident knowledge of detail; lastly, we had to look for that power combined with beauty that makes a great and noble building. In the set of drawings marked No. 1 (submitted by Mr G. Gilbert Scott) we find these qualities pre-eminently shown; we cannot but give it the first place.'

All the drawings had been exhibited in the Walker Art Gallery where the public could view them. But the cathedral committee had made it clear that they did not feel obliged to accept the assessors' recommendations. Most members were against Scott. They lacked confidence in such youth, despite what is called a good pedigree.

His grandfather, Sir Gilbert Scott (1810–77), was himself the grandson of the Calvinist Thomas Scott. His father was a Buckinghamshire clergyman. Young Gilbert began his career as a designer of workhouses, before being strongly attracted to the Gothic revival begun by the elder Pugin. He ended up by building churches and public buildings and restoring cathedrals at Ely, Hereford, Lichfield, Salisbury, Ripon, Chester, Worcester, Chichester, Gloucester, Rochester, and Exeter. As architect to the Dean and Chapter of Westminster Abbey, he was to restore that great national church and earn himself the distinction of being buried near to so many other famous bones.

He designed the hotel at St Pancras Station, the Albert Memorial, Glasgow University, and much else. But the Prime Minister, Lord Palmerston, would not allow him to do a Gothic Foreign Office in Whitehall. It prompted Palmerston to remark: 'Architects are persons who require to be kept under the strictest control.' Probably Gilbert Scott wouldn't have cared twopence for such a rebuke: during his career he added nearly 800 buildings to Britain's heritage. His elder son, George Gilbert Scott, carried the torch of the Gothic revival with greater agility and was more individualistic in approach. This regard for the 'old work', spliced with an ability for freshness of presentation, was inherited by Giles.

The application and impact of the Scotts in their various callings and professions prompted Sir John Betjeman to conclude that they 'probably had more influence in the last two centuries than any other family in England'. The cathedral committee were not so inclined to eulogize. A compromise was found. If Scott was to be retained, then Bodley must work with him and have joint status.

In the next chapter we shall look more closely at this partnership and its significance, but first it is essential to 'get inside the mind' of the cathedral's prime creator. When the foundation stone was laid in 1904, Scott wrote a most reveal-ing article for a *Liverpool Daily Post and Echo* supplement on the cathedral. It shows better than anything else his ideas on cathedral building. It is frank, critical, objective, and instructive. And although Scott was writing at a time when his earlier plans were in force, what he says applies equally to the qualities of the present building.

The condensed version of Scott's article reproduced here can be regarded as a fundamental essay on his methods: 'The building of a cathedral church is at any time an event which creates a flutter in the architectural world, but there is no concealing the fact that when a cathedral is to be built of such vast proportions as that contemplated for Liverpool, we have an event which is epoch-making in the history of English architecture.

'The all-important question of style in our present-day architecture is constantly discussed among architects, and when a work of this magnitude is undertaken, the discussion becomes doubly keen, a fact which in itself speaks volumes for, rather than against, the state of modern architectural style.

'It is curious living in a time considered by ourselves to be the most advanced and progressive, that the arts have nevertheless fallen from their high estate. We claim acquaintance with the styles of all ages and nationalities; we have studied their history and development, traced each step as they advanced, and having made this post mortem examination, we set to work and produce buildings that for ugliness are not approached by any buildings of past ages.

'There is, however, some consolation in the fact that so much progress has been made in the last fifty years. But we are still far from having a distinctive nationalistic style, and it is a thousand pities that such a state of things should exist at the present time, for this is undoubtedly a period of extraordinary building activity, which has no parallel in the nation's history.

'Many people knowing nothing of architecture said: "Let us have, in Liverpool Cathedral, something entirely new, a new style of architecture altogether." These people lose sight·of the fact that no new style of architecture has ever come suddenly into existence and flourished.

'Is there the slightest possibility that when a building like

Liverpool Cathedral is contemplated, a new and original style will suddenly come into existence, a style which is not only original, but—what is more important—beautiful? To some the latter seems only a secondary consideration, and their frantic efforts to attain originality at the expense of beauty is really pathetic.

'As there is no uniform style to which we can swear allegiance, each man thinks for himself and works in the particular style with which he is most in sympathy. Liverpool will have a Gothic cathedral, but of a quite different type to that of our medieval cathedrals; in fact, there is no Gothic building in the world to which it can be compared.

'We have, as a matter of fact, gone back to the beginning and struck out in a new direction.

'The traditions of Gothic have been destroyed, and we cannot get much further if we merely attempt to carry on the style from where the medievalists broke off. We can only study the style, and having grasped its spirit, we can then impart to it our own personality.

'One of the most hopeful signs in modern architecture is the growing appreciation of simplicity. There are still architects, however, who would like to see Liverpool Cathedral bristling with crocketed spires and pinnacles, but these are mostly men of the old school, the last of the original Gothic revivalists.

'We are beginning to see that we cannot nowadays do rich work if we wish to; carving seems a dead art, the stone is worked in a hard mechanical manner quite foreign to the real spirit of the Gothic; and another fact—the cost of labour—must be taken into account. All these are gradually driving us to simplicity, and as a result, architecture is fast improving.

'Liverpool Cathedral should not be a medieval cathedral dished up. True art does not allow copying. We may look through book after book to get ideas, but a true artist will always end up by throwing the books aside, and starting with a clean sheet of paper, will find his brain to be, after all, the best book of reference.

'Several abstract ideas were decided upon from the beginning, which would apply to whatever style was adopted.

Serious, sober, deeply earnest.
[s]omberly or gravely impressive.
Invoking the force of a religion.

Solemnity was to be the keynote of the design and this includes dignity, grandeur, and simplicity. The effect aimed at was to be obtained by the massing, grouping, and proportion of the various parts, and not by prettiness and luxuriance of detail. No amount of rich ornament can equal the beauty and charm of a blank wall, relieved by a touch—but only a touch—of rich detail. The lack of blank wall is perhaps the least satisfactory feature of our fine old cathedrals, for even when there is no profusion of canopy work, wall arcading, or stone panelling, we find that each bay has large traceried windows which almost fill the wall space between the buttresses, and as a result we have a lack of contrast which is of vital importance.

'All architecture should be strong, manly, and yet refined, but the combination of these qualities is not by any means easy to attain. Strength with coarseness is easily got, so is refinement with feebleness, but the combination of strength and refinement is the very highest ideal in architecture as in the other arts.

'In designing a modern cathedral, the treatment of the central space is the first problem to be solved, and we must consider this before attempting to work out the other parts. The central part should be designed to form the predominating feature inside and out.

'The distribution of light, the arrangement of light contrasts, and the lighting effects generally, have to be carefully considered throughout the cathedral. Mystery is a very important factor in design, and any large church will look fine inside if it is mysterious and gloomy, not, of course, depressingly gloomy, but with the dark parts arranged to come in contrast with the well-lighted portions.

'Most of our large medieval churches lack gloom; an exception, however, is Westminster Abbey, acknowledged to be the finest interior in the kingdom.

'The vaulting of Liverpool Cathedral will not be of the usual Gothic form, which is considered too light and intricate to give the solemn effect at which we are aiming, and the principal parts will be barrel vaulted.

'In designing this cathedral, an important factor in the working out has been a desire to make it interesting. Lack of interest in the majority of buildings put up nowadays has no doubt been responsible for the forced and affected originality which characterizes a great deal of modern architecture. Liverpool will have a cathedral which bears no resemblance to any other in the world, and if the citizens of this great port succeed, as no doubt they will, in completing the huge fabric, they will indeed have good cause for pride.'

In later years, when taking architects and students on tours of his emerging masterpiece, Scott would emphasize the openness of the concept with the repeated remark: 'Don't look at my arches, or the tracery of the windows, or the carved ornamentation; look at my spaces.' It will be seen that Scott was no plagiarist. He was, and remained, an individual working under the influence of the past.

The question of classifying Liverpool Cathedral's style has always caused problems. Vere Cotton said that the result was 'classic rather than Gothic', and went on: 'But if the bones are classic, then the flesh which clothes them is pure Gothic, even if it does not conform strictly to any of the recognized Gothic periods.'

Latterly, Scott himself was said to favour the phrase coined by an American visitor who called the style 'Space Gothic'. But whatever definition one strives for, the word Gothic must play a part. The whole force of its tradition has been to satisfy ecclesiastical needs, although there were later offshoots in the municipal, industrial, and domestic fields in an effort to make buildings 'worthy'.

In thirteenth-century Europe, Gothic began to symbolize the autonomy of the Church within the corporate life of the community. One great building inspired another, but as Scott noted in his article, forced originality never paid dividends. The fallacies of passing fashion had no place in the minds of those who fashioned the choir of Beauvais, or Amiens Cathedral, or the lantern at Ely.

In this country Norman preceded Gothic, as at Durham Cathedral, with the round arch imitated from the Roman buildings and with added barbaric ornamentation. Durham was for centuries the richest see in England, and its minster is in the Norman style, but in the Chapel of the Nine Altars came the introduction of Gothic architecture with the pointed arch, seen to perfection at Salisbury Cathedral. This was preferred because it allowed the use of narrow windows side by side, which in the days before the 'rediscovery' of glass-making, were often hung with shutters which opened and closed like Venetian blinds.

Later, when glass manufacture and staining were again firmly to the fore, windows were made large and broad and enhanced with delicate stone tracery. This, and the contemporary taste for sculpture and carving, formed the Decorated style. Thus cathedral builders invariably adopted the newest ideas in art and architecture, so much so that their work can be dated by its style.

Eventually, in the late seventeenth century, the final stages of compromise were reached. The refinements of Sir Christopher Wren and his successors would have been impossible in the Middle Ages, just as the true knowledge of Gothic art could not be revived on demand. Yet Gothic architecture does take on a 'permanence' as it progresses. Scott once said: 'It does not allow you to complete the fabric before adding detail, as detail is part of the fabric, the ornament part of the structure. It is not like Westminster Cathedral, where you can build a plain shell and cover it with marble and mosaics afterwards.'

Whereas a feeling of spontaneity within such limitations has always been important, one of the prime considerations of the architect must be an ability to inspire his collaborators. This is a gift which Scott never ceased to use. The late E. Carter Preston, who sculptured among other items the figures which adorn the Nave, gave a valuable indication of the rapport which existed between Scott and the artists who brought the building to fruition.

In a wartime letter he said: 'Sir Giles has often invited us to discuss and talk over with him the special problems as they have arisen.... I shall always remember one occasion when he took us into his confidence on the matter of his working: he said the problem haunted his mind, but was cluttered with vague and chaotic frillings which prevented the emergence of the true sensation. He would wrestle with these false motives, trying to sieve from them the core of his idea. Eventually, he would give up the struggle, feeling that his idea was not so intense as he at first thought, or it would find its solution more readily, whereupon he would put the whole thing out of his conscious mind and a few days—or possibly weeks later—he found, to his surprise, the idea presented itself to him clothed in its true form, asking to be materialized.'

Carter Preston reported that a particularly interesting discussion concerned the West Fronts of English cathedrals. 'He thought that some of our most cherished cathedrals cast their spell over us because of their lovely colour or charming surroundings, rather than through eloquent design or truly resolved forms. . . . We live in excited anticipation, knowing that the achievement will be beyond our most ambitious flights of fancy: something new and strange, yet making concrete our latent desires in a manner more intense than we can conceive, a thing to be perpetually explored and a continuous delight in discovery.

'It is true that we workers have found joy in the doing of our several parts and joy in the knowing that when the various portions are assembled that a great work of art will be born, not something to be stuffed into an art gallery or museum, but a thing that is part and parcel of our daily lives.'

If Scott could achieve such acclaim from his co-workers, he was nevertheless reluctant to delegate even a tug on the reins of real authority to anyone else. Over the years he produced many large-scale drawings of the building, all by his own hand.

Liverpool Cathedral became the *cause célèbre* of his life. His aim, he once said, had been to approach the project as a modeller rather than as a draughtsman. But there was an element of sadness in his early realization that the cathedral would mark the end of a style he loved so much. Shortly after he won the design competition, he told a Liverpool School of

Architecture class: 'Time alone will show whether this building is the last flare-up of the Gothic revival.' In time, he had to admit that it was.

Yet Scott lived to be honoured not merely by the bestowal of a knighthood in 1924 or the thrill in 1942 of placing in position the highest stone on the tower, but, in a real way, by the recognition of contemporaries in his field and beyond. In January 1943, when the crown of the tower was being revealed, a special tribute luncheon was held at Liverpool's Stork Hotel. There, A. E. Richardson, Professor of Architecture at London University, told Scott: 'Your magnificent cathedral is symbolic of the national pride and thoroughness. It is something that everybody can understand. It has a familiarity of mass which is inspiring. It is highly original, yet not strangely so. Its theme epitomizes an ancient and wonderful civilization. All that is embodied in the old cathedrals, abbeys, and churches is reached anew.

'. . . It is not mock Gothic, its prototype does not exist in a pattern book. Although the continent of Europe can show antique ecclesiastical buildings of great scale and fantastic outline, it is significant that few modern works of similar scope exhibit the true principles of stereotomy.'

In a message delivered at the same function, John Masefield, then Poet Laureate, had written: 'This cathedral of Liverpool, the greatest of modern cathedrals, is a church of the Resurrection. It comes into the life of our time, in a decade when all the ways of life known to us from childhood have to be re-made, when the nation has to be re-created, with what difficulty we do not yet know, but no doubt with much.

'This cathedral, therefore, should be the symbol of that Resurrection, and at the same time its standard. What has been muffled and in shrouds and buried down deep after being broken by the soldiers, should emerge here and be triumphant. Then, indeed, it would be a cathedral that Is and Is as it should be.'

That same month, however, there were also some harsh words about his design. The cathedral was referred to as 'dreadful' in a BBC Brains Trust broadcast. Asked for comment, Sir Giles told a *Liverpool Daily Post* reporter: 'I have so seldom heard a word of condemnation of the cathedral that I experienced a feeling of almost relief.'

But there was a sting to be added: 'Some people have a robot, mechanical outlook on architecture, and only like architectural expressions that agree with that mental outlook. Their view is that buildings should look like a machine, and should give the impression of being functional, even if they don't always function.'

Scott was never one to be put down or deterred from his purpose by a handful of critics. His single-minded determination to achieve a cathedral of unsurpassed stature in a new century was to beat them all. Alas, the man who built a cathedral to last for a thousand years died in February 1960. For nearly sixty years he had been a constant visitor— imagining, planning, watching, and discussing. In the April journal of the Royal Institute of British Architects, Sir Hugh Worthington, a friend of his, wrote: 'By the death of Sir Giles Scott we have lost our greatest architect of achievement, and a man of outstanding and lovable character.' Scott was, Worthington continued, 'a singularly beautiful character, free of the jealousies that so often spoil the successful artist. He bore life's triumphs and life's trials with an unruffled serenity. Time will prove the enduring value of his contribution to English architecture and his many friends will mourn his loss.'

At the cathedral, Dean Dillistone added his own tribute: 'The name Giles Scott will ever be associated with the cathedral. There can be few great buildings in the whole history of mankind that have been so completely the outcome of one man's genius.'

Scott's ashes were interred at a point to lie beneath the great western front of the cathedral on its completion. (Ironically, because of costs, the original plans for the façade had to be changed after Scott's death.)

The Dean and Chapter decided to remember their architect in the manner of so many other great European cathedrals, by 'central recognition'. At Chartres, Amiens, and elsewhere the names of the architects had been set in the floor; at Rheims, a labyrinth was incised forming a maze which led to a central memorial. At Liverpool, Scott's son Richard, also an architect, designed a tribute, which was laid in the floor beneath the tower vault. It is most fitting that anyone who now stands at the mid-point of the cathedral and looks up to the great height of the Te Deum or Benedicite Windows, will remember a man who dared to conceive such an enterprise, and which in itself is his most noble monument.

The other great revelation, which so many people are still unaware of, is that Scott was a Roman Catholic.

4

Building Blocks

> Scott was more of an artist than an architect. In
> Gothic architecture, the perpendicular wins over the
> horizontal to throw the eyes upward. . . . It's a great
> building. I'm proud to have worked on it.
>
> TOMMY ROWBOTTOM

Men no longer fashion their cathedrals from the raw rock of
creation. This is the era of concrete and steel or factory brick.
But Liverpool Cathedral is different: like Durham, Lincoln,
York, Salisbury, and the ancient mother churches, it is a
stonemason's cathedral, largely built by the hands of men who
are at the end of a long and historic line of craft technique.
And although Europe and America are showing a renewed
interest in building with stone, no project will again match
Liverpool Cathedral for size.

When a visitor comes to the cathedral, he is at once
impressed by how detail has been worked within enormity. He
sees nothing which is shoddy. Scott, the magician, persuades
against any preconceptions. Many of our churches are
marred by the thoughtless introduction of unartistic, machine-
made ornaments, by senseless decoration, and by colours
which clash and vulgarize. The ordinary parish church cannot
afford, in most cases, to provide either the quality or quantity
of workmanship which was aimed at here, where art is the
handmaid of worship.

Stained-glass artists, engineers, glaziers, embroiderers,
carpenters, and joiners have all played their part. But surely
none of these would deny that, primarily, Liverpool Cathedral
is a monument to the stonemasons who created the grand
shell which houses all those other crafts. You can read the
stones like you can read signatures. The marks of the finishing
tools are as distinctive as a painter's brushstrokes.

Giles Scott once said that he wanted the stone left as the
masons had finished it. He did not mind if in some places it

3 Liverpool Cathedral belongs to the stonemasons and will be the last great building in Britain on which they do new work.

was rougher than others; that only added to the character of the place. Yet he sometimes thought that he had designed impossibilities for his builders. For instance, at one point, three arches meet in a T, and the mouldings run through the junction in a complicated cross-over. One thoughtless chisel blow would have ruined the whole enterprise. All the stones were shaped separately on the site. Each was then numbered and within days was put into position. Some types of work would never be repeated, so it stretched the masons' abilities and challenged them (a Texan visitor, who thought that the stonework was imported from Italy, was promptly marched to the masons' yard to be enlightened at first hand!). It was a traditional craft in which sons followed fathers, as in the mining communities of Wales and the factories of industrial Lancashire. In fact, until the Second World War, only the sons of established masons would be considered for training.

In the 1930s more than 200 men were employed on the

cathedral site; of these 120 were masons. By 1978 that work-force, drastically reduced all round, included only three full-time masons on site. Over the years the numbers had de-creased because of new methods of construction and stone-cutting. The old mallet and chisel, formerly obligatory for apprentices up to eighteen, gradually gave way to pneumatic chisels. Before 1949, when the power tools were introduced, everything except the sawing of stone had to be done by hand. The advent of mechanization was regarded with apprehension by some masons, but it certainly speeded up the building process, and in 1954 the first moulding and planing machines came into use. The circular cutting saws, with teeth of 87 per cent diamond dust, steel, and tungsten, could pass through stone at the rate of 2 ft per minute.

There was even the suggestion that if mechanization had been used earlier, the cost and time involved in building the cathedral might have been dramatically cut back. In 1968, L. T. H. Rumsay, the President of the British Stone Federa-tion, wrote to the *Liverpool Echo*, saying that cutting machines had been around for a century. Had they been used when the cathedral was started, the work could have been done in half the time at a third of the price. That is an issue which future historians may wish to debate. But they should also note that after 1934, the quarries at Woolton, which yielded the red sandstone, were given to the cathedral by the Marquess of Salisbury, thus representing a substantial 'invisible' contribu-tion to the building funds.

Such costing formulae were not the concern of the masons themselves: men like Tommy Rowbottom, who joined the workforce in 1932 as a lad of sixteen and stayed until the last stone was placed in position. His qualities have been a good eye, a strong arm, and an ability to see how his work fitted into the overall design. When he arrived, the builders were up to the Rose Window height of the Central Space. During the forty-six years of construction that followed, Tommy's achievements included tracery work and two pinnacles on the tower; working stone for the porches of the Central Space; fixing the Nave bridge in position; and setting the stones for the greater part of the Nave. His main challenge, he says, was fixing the groin ceiling in the Nave—an aspect of masonry that will never be called for again.

He tells you that he is not a religious man, but adds with pride that he has 'helped to place the stone as God made it, to create the largest single uninterrupted space in the world'.

The financial rewards were never great. As an apprentice he received the equivalent of 8p a week; by the time the cathedral was completed, the top-line rate was 'around £60 a week'.

'Masonry has never paid. I sometimes used to say that if I had my time over again, I would do something else. However, I don't think that is particularly true. It gets into your blood. But like the builders of Solomon's Temple, there is something in that saying that "ye shall go ragged and weary to the end of thy days".'

Like all true craftsmen and artists, Tommy Rowbottom's reward has been in seeing his work materialize. And he tells fascinating stories of how Scott would have parts of the emerging building taken down and rebuilt. 'That was his way of calling the committee's bluff. One example is the Choir Aisle wall opposite the entrance to the Lady Chapel. At first it was plain. Then it was redone with extra detail in it.'

For a working man with no pretensions, Tommy can equally astonish with his eloquence of opinion: 'Scott was more of an artist than an architect. In Gothic architecture, the perpendicular wins over the horizontal, to throw the eyes upward. . . .' He is also of the opinion that the building committee had let themselves down at the final hurdle, by having concrete roofs for the Nave triforium vaulting and some fibreglass facing for the fabric. 'You save costs in one direction and other problems arise.'

For all that, his lifetime's work has been worth while and will outlast the work of scores of other more famous men. 'It is a great building. I'm proud to have worked on it.'

It is an enterprise which has occupied many minds over the years. The decision to build a cathedral on St James's Mount was truly monumental. Liverpool was about to provide England's Northern Province with its first mother church since the Reformation. Just thirty-one years before Scott's design was accepted, the Bishop of Carlisle, Dr Goodwin, had written: 'We build parish churches day by day . . . but we never, in England at least, build a cathedral, and if we did, no one would venture to design a structure such as those which the medieval architects have left us; nor is there any probability that any conjunction of circumstances will in future make such a thing possible. . . . We may as well expect another *Iliad* from a Greek poet as another cathedral from an English architect.'

Other dioceses had been prepared to upgrade and embellish parish churches. Not Liverpool. And now, even the sceptics who had thought the adventure terminated when Emerson's 'Dome' cathedral plans had been shelved in Bishop Ryle's time, were to be confounded. Liverpool was to set its cathedral on high ground formed from the rubble of a former quarry—a site with an interesting story of its own. For the quarry, which contained Liverpool 'Spa', was later to be a cemetery and then public gardens.

John Wood the Younger, of Bath, chose to use the Keuper sandstone from here for building Liverpool Town Hall. The quarry also provided most of the material for Liverpool Parish Church (the steeple and main body of which has since been rebuilt). Latterly, the unemployed were put to work in piling up the quarry debris on which the cathedral stands.

The spring, which still flows out of a wall on the east of the site, first came to prominence in 1773, when James Worthington, a local surgeon, published a paper commending the waters for 'loss of appetite, nerve disorders, lowness of spirits, headaches, rickets, and sore eyes'. The 'flat, slightly iron-tinted' flavour of Liverpool Spa—the source of which is still unknown—was also said to cure rheumatics. An inscription near the spring read: 'Christian reader, view in me, An emblem of true charity, And I have full return from Heaven, For every cup of water given.' Taking the waters became fashionable. Specialists in nearby Rodney Street sent patients there. The place was fully credited with healing powers but never declared holy! Thousands of people came from all over Lancashire to fill up their bottles at the spring.

In February 1825, when no more stone was being excavated, the place was turned into a cemetery and named after St James's Church, Toxteth. Between June of that year and July 1936, when the last interment took place, nearly 58,000 people were buried there. Here lie the remains of Sarah Biffen, the limbless artist whose royal patrons included George III, George IV, William IV, and Queen Victoria; William Lynn, the Aintree landlord who is said to have initiated the Grand National; Captain William Harrison, who commanded the *Great Eastern*; Captain John Oliver, who served with Nelson on HMS *Victory*; and Kitty Wilkinson, who founded Britain's first washhouse after the cholera epidemic of the 1830s. But the most famous soul at rest is the Rt Hon William ('Free Trade') Huskisson, MP for Liverpool, who had the dubious distinction of being the first person to be killed by a train: he was mown down by Stephenson's 'Rocket' at the opening of the Liverpool to Manchester Railway. The circular mausoleum to him, in the style of a small classical temple, can still be seen.

Another interesting building associated with the cemetery, and now within the cathedral confines, is a tiny Grecian chapel, designed by John Foster Jnr. It stands dwarfed by the Nave Entrance and Benedicite Window of its neighbour. Formerly used as a shelter for mourners and coffins, it was Foster's smallest building. The cathedral committee decided it should remain when the cemetery was closed, and Scott himself described it as the 'perfect foil' to the cathedral's size.

The cemetery site eventually became overgrown and provided an unofficial adventure playground for local children. But the vandalism to vaults and gravestones became a major problem. Then in 1971, after a transformation which took three years, it was reopened as Cathedral Gardens, with the headstones from the graves lining the perimeter. Some would have preferred to see it remain wild. In his book *Seaport* Quentin Hughes says: 'It should be left as it is; a place for contemplation and poetic inspiration.' But with the cathedral now finished, nobody could seriously contend that it would have been better forsaken in a vandalized state. This aspect of the cathedral is the most splendid, at least until the other surrounding areas are properly townscaped.   •

Scott recognized the potential of the man-made ravine below, in heightening (literally) the drama of the cathedral building. His competition drawing showed a church with an overall length of 450 ft; a transept width of 198 ft; nave vaulting of 116 ft; and two main towers each of 260 ft.

Despite the remarks he made in his essay of 1904, the exterior was decked with almost wedding-cake detail and fussiness of line, and the use of glass had little vertical stress compared with the eventual result. But within a year of the appointment of Scott and Bodley as joint architects in 1903, a completely new plan emerged. Scott was still keen on the idea of twin towers as the dominating feature, but the most notable change was that the Lady Chapel had moved from its original (and traditional) position behind the High Altar, to become an extended finger on the south-east part of the design. Other changes included lengthening the Nave and giving a new look to the West End and entrances.

The result, Scott concluded, was 'neither Bodley's nor mine'. Changes in the competition design, with the elder man 'altering a bit here and a bit there', dissatisfied and annoyed Scott. He obviously regarded Bodley as an *éminence grise*. Their relationship was heading for disaster.

But work had already started on the 1904 plan. Contracts for the first part of the project had been placed. Expensive foundations had been dug down to the bedrock up to 50 ft below. Everyone except Scott (and perhaps Bodley) was in celebratory mood. On 19 July 1904, King Edward VII and Queen Alexandra came to lay the Foundation Stone—itself a gift from the Mothers' Meetings throughout the diocese. At St James's Mount, a huge amphitheatre had been erected to hold 8,000 people. The King told Merseysiders: 'I am convinced that the cathedral will minister to the spiritual needs of this great community and will form a noble addition to the architectural adornments of your city.'

4   The laying of the Foundation Stone by King Edward VII and
    Queen Alexandra, 19 July 1904.

In parallel, the church establishment was busy issuing good
tidings. Bishop Chavasse, in a message from his palace,
declared: 'It is my earnest desire that the new cathedral of
Liverpool shall be built by all and for all; that it shall be the
church of the people, where rich and poor shall meet together
to worship God, and where the gospel of our Lord Jesus
Christ is fully preached. It must be the best that we can give,
and its walls and towers rising high above the city must be a
silent but majestic witness to God and the unseen.'

On the surface there was good reason for cheer. Plenty of
cash had been flowing in for the launching of the project. Even
before the design had been chosen, £144,000 was in the kitty.
By the midsummer of 1903, the figure was as high as £170,000.
Two years earlier, Lord Derby had set the tone of the appeal
with the clichéd, if effective, assertion that those who gave
little should be able to feel personal involvement equal to that
of people who donated great amounts.

The cathedral was to be built in 'blocks'—each portion

completed before the next was begun. Because the work depended on donations, and because it was a long-term project, no set price could even be guessed at. Subsequently over the years, estimates on cost and timing, although based on seemingly reliable information, had almost always proved to be wildly incorrect. For instance, in 1938, Vere Cotton in an article for *Country Life* magazine, said that the total cost of building was likely to be in the region of £2½ million (at that time £1½ million had been spent). And in 1944, Colonel Alan Tod, chairman of the cathedral's executive committee, said that it would take another decade to complete the building.

Such examples alone show that the realization of the cathedral dream has had to be undertaken literally on a day-to-day basis. But there were to be many great milestones along the way, as each portion was started and completed.

In 1906 the Foundation Stone of the Chapter House was laid by the Duke of Connaught. Here was more pomp and ceremony to steal the limelight from the vital issue seething beneath—the incompatibility of Bodley and Scott.

The Americans had asked Bodley to plan a new cathedral in Washington. To avoid any undue turmoil in committee over whether Liverpool would continue to receive the right share of his attentions, the clerk of works was told that all plans must bear the signature of both architects. But the following year, Bodley's status changed from that of joint to consultant architect. He would still look after his chief interests such as ornaments and stained glass, while he would also be expected to approve Scott's plans. Yet even this was not enough to appease the up-and-coming prodigy. Scott had shed his milk teeth and decided to bite hard. He wrote out his resignation—a move which at least showed that he had the strategic muscle to match a committee which had not particularly favoured him from the beginning. But as fate would have it, Bodley died before Scott's letter reached the cathedral committee.

We enter the realms of pure conjecture if we try to imagine what would have happened if Scott had gone and Bodley had lived on. However, it would be amiss if the older man's role in

5 The charming intimacy of the Lady Chapel, the first part of
the building to be completed.

the cathedral story is not seen in its true context. He made a very real contribution to the style of the Lady Chapel, having worked with Scott for four of the seven years which that part of the building took. This was the embryo of the cathedral as it is today, yet showing Bodley's more ornate influence. Vere Cotton summed it up precisely when he wrote that the Lady Chapel was a 'composition in line', while the Choir was a 'composition in mass'.

There are other important considerations too. Along with Norman Shaw, it was Bodley who had chosen Scott in the first place; if he had not assumed the role of joint architect, Scott would not have been employed. Neither should the resulting friction be seen as an act of youthful truculence on the part of Scott; nor should it imply that Scott was ungrateful to Bodley. The simple truth is that Scott was an 'all-or-nothing' creator who passionately believed in his own ideas and did not wish to see them tampered with. One must presume, therefore, that the frustrations were mutual.

But even after Bodley's death, the overall project was not too far advanced for a change of helmsman to be out of the question. As it was, the cathedral committee seemed to hold a new faith in Scott which, to their credit, was to be proved.

Scott virtually began all over again on the main part of the building. Towards the end of 1910, the central portion was given a new treatment to provide a great congregational space which had been missing from the original design. The twin tower idea which had overshadowed the first two conceptions was scrapped, and a central tower 20 ft higher was substituted. This allowed for a vast middle area in the cathedral, measuring 190ft by 81ft. By some miracle the committee agreed that Scott should take sole charge and they accepted his proposals.

When Sir Christopher Wren had been given final approval for his second design for St Paul's, it is recorded that he 'got the King to give him permission to alter it as much as he liked, without showing models or drawings to anyone'. Scott's ploy was to convince, where Wren had decided to dictate. As Vere Cotton has remarked: 'There can be few other instances in history of a building committee so readily acquiescing in changes, often liable to involve both delay and expense.'

But obviously there were some pockets of disquiet. Was this change for change's sake? Bishop Chavasse was there to calm any brewing storm. The *Diocesan Gazette* reported: 'There is no doubt that this change of plans has occasioned considerable surprise and no little criticism in the diocese and out of it, but the Bishop is convinced that once the public are in full possession of all the facts, and are able to compare the new design with the old, the action of the committee will be fully justified.'

One of the great boasts of Liverpool Cathedral's story is that once building work began, it was virtually continuous even during two world wars. So while Scott and Bodley had been at loggerheads and while the new plan was emerging and the committee were deliberating, the column bases of the original design had been sunk into position. Therefore, Scott had to tailor his latest vision to fit in with what had already been accomplished.

The usual positioning for a single great tower in a Gothic cathedral had been where the transepts—Nave and Choir—join: the intersection of the traditional cross-shaped ground plan. Here, the space between where the twin towers were to have been built was not large enough for the size of tower the architect now wanted. He decided to plan it farther west and to balance the whole with another set of transepts. (It is from this new plan that the idea for the arms of the later Dean and Chapter, with its 'double cross' emblem, came.) Whereas most cathedrals had a main east-west architectural progression of Choir–Transept–Nave, Liverpool had evolved to become Choir–First Transept–Central Space (Undertower)–Second Transept–Nave. The site just—and only just—allowed for a Nave of the same length as the Choir. Again, geography set the main entrances in the centre rather than at the west. The plan was now classical, symmetrical about both axes.

Scott was evidently pleased with his new baby. He recalled: 'My command of my medium undoubtedly improved as time went on . . . I obtained, in fact, a far greater command of the third dimension.'

The cathedral committee had decided to make the completion of the Lady Chapel their first objective. This would give Liverpool a 'mini-cathedral' while the Choir of the main building was being erected. And so it was that on St Peter's Day, 29 June 1910, the Lady Chapel was consecrated. St Peter's Pro-Cathedral could now be demolished and St Nicholas's could become the parish church.

The Lady Chapel, the Chapter House, and the initial stages of work on the Choir had cost nearly £760,000. It was a lot of money, but a great deal more would be needed. The new design from Scott had not dented enthusiasm for the project; on the contrary, many people were more attracted by the provision of a great Central Space. But from time to time it was necessary to be seen to talk about the grand plan as well as to be carrying it out. In 1911, Bishop Chavasse had this to say about the cathedral's role: 'In a community set on money-making, the spiritual is in special danger of being forgotten in the temporal, and the seen is perilously apt to stifle the thought of the unseen. A man's ambitions become bounded by the horizon of this world, and the idea of God slowly fades out of his heart.

'The work is great, for the palace is not for man, but for the Lord God. The cost is tremendous, for it must worthily represent the wealth, the influence, and the devotion of a powerful diocese. It will call for sustained and widespread self-sacrifice and co-operation. But the end is glorious. If as a diocese we set our affection to the House of our God, if we forget our differences, our jealousies, our prejudices, and are caught in the great and strong current of the love of God, which sets us towards glorifying Him by building a holy and beautiful house for His sanctuary, faith and love will triumph over our every difficulty, and ultimate success is sure. And when we pass away, and our place knows us no more, we shall leave behind the beginnings, at any rate, of a noble pile, which by its impressive grandeur will witness for God, and which by its manifold uses will help to spiritualize the life of a great community and preserve the faith as it is in Jesus, for our children and our children's children.'

It was just the sort of religious and emotional uplift that bishops specialize in. And there were hard times just around the corner. By 1914, £441,000 had spilled into the cathedral coffers, of which £333,000 had already spilled out and been converted into fees, wages, and masonry. There wasn't much left, but as if in defiance of the carnage of war, the committee decided to carry on building. To stop might be to threaten the whole operation, dull the impetus, and lose for ever the skills and crafts being regenerated on the site.

When building became fully in operation again in 1920, the whole financial complexion of the scheme had changed. The fund raisers began to experience the first real taste of a thing called inflation which was to dog them until the last stone was laid fifty-eight years later.

Cathedrals, like any other institution, need to be in the news for people to sit up and take notice. News has always been defined as the unusual or extraordinary, and the day-to-day construction of Liverpool Cathedral had long ceased to be newsworthy. The next bout of headlines did not come until 1924 when the Choir and the Eastern Transept were consecrated. This provided for the first real glimpse of the grand interior—the promise of what was to come, a church interior exceeded in area only by St Peter's (Rome), Milan Cathedral, Seville Cathedral, and St John the Divine (New York).

King George V suggested that the official ceremony should take place on 19 July, the twentieth anniversary of the laying of the Foundation Stone. He attended in full state with Queen Mary and eight archbishops and forty-five bishops from all over the world. It was a day to remember, particularly for the *enfant terrible* turned architectural hero, Giles Scott. That day, at a private ceremony at Lord Derby's home, Knowsley Hall, he became Sir Giles. The King and Queen also attended the dedication of the War Memorial Chapel and Cenotaph before returning to London. It is interesting to note that this was the first cenotaph to be suggested in Britain as a memorial to the fallen of the First World War. (Little more than twenty

6   The Choir of the cathedral begins to emerge on the skyline above St James's Cemetery, now Cathedral Gardens.

years later it would also be a place of remembrance for members of the merchant and fishing fleets who died in the Second World War.)

Meanwhile writers, commentators, and the public at large were beginning to take note of Liverpool's newest—and greatest—building. The Lady Chapel, Chapter House, and Choir provided several points for comment.

The overriding feature of the exterior was the prominence of the buttressing, which was duplicated on the Choir interior. This had the effect of 'screening' the influx of light into the building and giving the mystery Scott so wished for. And there was the great Te Deum Window, designed to catch the rising sun on Christmas morning. This huge window, 76 ft by 44 ft, was of such proportions that it would have been possible for the whole of the Lady Chapel to be passed through it. On the other hand, the octagonal Chapter House was a humbler feature, for there was no need to build one on the scale seen in the medieval cathedrals of York and elsewhere. The Dean and Chapter of Liverpool, when formed, would not be nearly so large.

Also noted were the French and Italian influences that had affected the conception of the Lady Chapel exterior; and the Spanish hallmarks in the design of the main cathedral reredos which, like the Bishop's Throne and the reredos of the War Memorial Chapel, was made from stone and formed part of the cathedral fabric.

Foreign influences (though realized in a completely original form) were to continue in the next section, the Undertower. In 1924, while riding high on a wave of actual accomplishment, an appeal was launched for £300,000. This was later increased by £50,000. The money would provide for the Central Space, the tower vault and the West Transept.

In many ways the tower and Central Space were to be the most exciting part of the venture. There would be nothing comparable in any other Gothic cathedral. (Alternative names suggested for the Central Space include the Naos, which is applied to the principal chamber or body of a temple, and the Middlerood, which has an Anglo-Saxon flavour.) The result has been an undertower of 72 ft square which, with the transept crossings on either side, gives 15,000 square feet of unobstructed vision. The tower rests on the outer walls of the building to the north and south and is supported within by two massive 107 ft arches, the highest Gothic arches ever built. The tower is the gift of the cathedral's greatest benefactors, the Vesteys. In 1934 Lord Vestey and his brother, Sir Edmund Vestey, gave £220,000 in memory of their parents, Samuel and Hannah Vestey, who were Southport business people. They later increased this to more than £266,000, and in 1953 the second Lord Vestey and Mr Ronald Vestey, their grandsons, brought the total to £301,000 to cover the entire cost of the tower building.

Scott was for many years preoccupied with the tower design, and the final one came after five earlier plans had been scrapped. The eventual height was 31 ft more than the 1910 drawings had shown and over 50 ft greater than that of the twin towers of the 1904 design. Its majesty and scale was to be the culminating feature of the exterior. Vere Cotton has rightly commented: 'The Vestey Tower can rank among the great towers of the world, not only by reason of its size, but for the beauty of its proportions and the subtlety of its modelling.' Two great technical feats distinguish its construction: the tapering lines which narrow off at a ratio of 1:80, and the concrete girdle which is fitted to the interior immediately above the vault, to withstand the stresses of the world's highest and heaviest ringing peal of bells.

The 'slimming' of the tower with height is known by architects as the art of 'battered verticals'. Scott admitted that he had never seen a book on the subject and said that it was something which had been ignored by those who wrote extensively on church building in the Victorian age. 'They never seemed to tumble to the subtlety of batter', was his famous remark, which sounded as if it had been coined from the script of a satire show.

The girdle, with more than 600 tons of concrete and 40 tons of reinforcements is 6 ft thick. The idea was to throw the stresses from the combined bell weight of 30 tons to the outer walls of the tower and as low down as possible.

The thirteen bells, grouped around a massive bourdon in its own concrete frame, were cast by the same firm that had made Big Ben for the Palace of Westminster. The largest, weighing $14\frac{1}{2}$ tons, was cast at Loughborough and among British bells is second only to the $16\frac{1}{2}$-ton Great Paul at St Paul's Cathedral. Liverpool's giant, called Great George, has a diameter of $9\frac{1}{2}$ ft and was hoisted into position through the bell trap in the centre of the tower vault—an operation which took several hours. The peal was first heard in 1951, when the Queen (then Princess Elizabeth) and Prince Philip came to open the Rankin Porch entrance on the south side of the Central Space.

Mention should also be made here of the cathedral's most distinctive 'voice': the five-manual organ, which at the time of its dedication in 1926 was the largest cathedral instrument ever built. With nearly 10,000 pipes ranging in length from less than 1 in to 32 ft, and with 145 speaking-stops, it began to

The largest bell, Great George, shortly before being hoisted to its position in the belfry.

attract a recital audience from all over the country, a success which has been continued. In size, the organ cases and pipe-work which occupy the Choir bays nearest the East Transept, were in keeping with what was being built farther west, and with the immensity of the scheme which was gradually unfolding.

The Central Space was taken into use in July 1941, after sixteen years of work. The last stone of the Vestey Tower was placed in position by Scott on 20 February 1942, on a pinnacle which was just one inch higher than the others. Once again, Liverpool was continuing and celebrating the building of its cathedral in the midst of war.

But as well as construction, there was destruction. On two consecutive nights in September 1940, the blitz which had wrecked so much of Liverpool's dockland and city centre inflicted its toll on the cathedral. A bomb which landed on the Founder's Plot (the burial place of Bishop Chavasse and his wife) blew out a dozen windows in the Lady Chapel and the

8   Giles Gilbert Scott (second from right) at the Topping Out
     ceremony on the tower, 20 February 1942.

south side of the Choir. Then in May the following year, the
cathedral works office was damaged and a bomb hit the
southern side of the East Transept. It struck a traverse arch
and fortunately was deflected into the street below. The previous November, King George VI and Queen Elizabeth had
visited Liverpool to express sympathy with those made homeless by the bombing. The King told the cathedral Chapter:
'Keep going, whatever you do, even if you can only go on in a
small way.'

When the bomb damage was repaired after the war, the
Choir windows were modified: narrower lancets, thinner
tracery, and lighter glazing had the effect of making the
interior brighter.

During the war, £89,000 had been given to the building
fund. Building licences were a necessity because of the

priority which had to be given to domestic and industrial rebuilding, and in 1948 the go-ahead was given for the starting of the first bay of the Nave. Seven years later, when the Lady Chapel was reopened, another appeal was launched for £500,000—the first appeal for more than thirty years. The same year, 1955, saw the tower officially taken over by the Dean and Chapter (during the building of the cathedral, it was always policy for the committee to hold responsibility for a section while it was under construction and for it to become the charge of the Dean only on completion).

Cathedral appeals have always met with a good initial response, but sustaining the inflow of money was a major challenge. By the end of 1955 £356,000 had been given but when the appeal account was closed in 1956, only £4,000 more had come in. As the new part of the cathedral grew day by day, so the first part of the building was increasingly in need of maintenance. In 1960 it was decided to give Cathedral Builders—a fund-raising body separate from the main appeal office—wider terms of reference. Since their inception in 1924, Cathedral Builders had raised more than £100,000 for the erection of the cathedral. Now their title was changed to the Friends and Builders, and the object was to have a representative in every parish to act as a link between the cathedral and local churches. The aim was to encourage small donors without detracting from those who wished to give large sums.

Taking stock of the overall situation as a new decade dawned, it was revealed that more than £2½ million had been spent on the cathedral, and of this nearly £500,000 had been earned from interest. However, costs and inflation were making nonsense of financial calculations and, as time went by, the fall in share values made the future uncertain. The cathedral committee had originally budgeted to spend £350,000 on the first bay of the Nave, but when the money was handed over in 1961, the real cost was counted at £420,000. People were beginning to question the final sum that would have to be spent if the cathedral was to be finished at all. The West Front designed by Scott would have to be

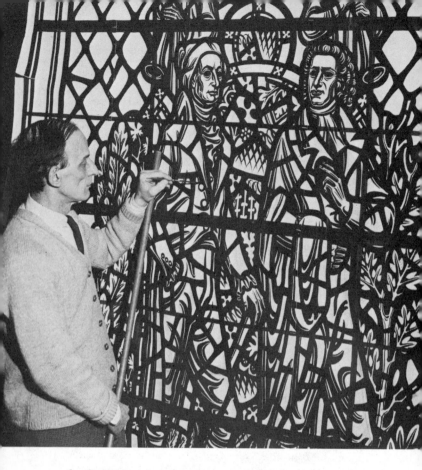

9 Carl Edwards, a stained-glass window artist, working on a
'cartoon' for the Benedicite Window at the West End of the
cathedral. The finished window covers 1,600 sq ft.

modified, they argued. Scott had produced five drawings over
the years, but his final plan, dating from 1942, was now
threatening to be too costly.

Frederick Thomas, a long-standing partner of Scott, produced a new and simplified design. In 1967 this was made
known to the public. It consisted of the same elements as the
East Front: twin buttresses, a high arch, and a great window.

But unlike the East Window (Te Deum) the West (Benedicite) was to be recessed from the face of the arch to give a dramatic shadow effect.

When the second bay of the Nave was almost finished, Dean Patey gave an assurance that the cathedral was not to be completed 'on the cheap'. He wrote in his summer newsletter: 'The West Front will have a directness and monumental quality entirely in harmony with Giles Scott's best work. There will be no falling away from the high quality of craftsmanship which has been such a notable feature of the whole operation.'

Two days after the second bay was opened, in May 1968, the Lord Mayor of Liverpool launched a £500,000 'Finish the Cathedral' appeal. The Dean said that the Nave was not just an 'expensive decoration'. He could use every inch of available space. Future generations would have cause to be thankful for such a superb instrument of worship. 'We can say with confidence: "The best is yet to be".'

At a news conference he stressed that the building was timeless. 'Architectural fashions may come and go, but I believe that in every century men and women of taste and sensitivity will look at our building and say: "This really is a cathedral."

'A Dean is neither the director of a building operation nor the curator of an ecclesiastical museum. He is a servant of the church of God. My job, in collaboration with my colleagues, is to use the cathedral as an instrument for the Kingdom of God. This is our yardstick.'

Within eight months the appeal had raised £300,000. There had been plenty of good will and practical action in the parishes, but the cathedral committee and the Dean were anxious that their fund raising should not disturb the ongoing commitments of the parishes. (This was in line with what Bishop Ryle had said more than half a century before.) The whole amount was raised by June 1971, but there was a warning of inflation from the chairman of the appeal committee.

Would there never be an end to their requests for aid?

There were more embarrassing issues too. During the course of the appeal, a protester had daubed a message in paint on the outside of the building: 'CHRIST WAS POOR AND HOMELESS. TWO THIRDS OF HUMANITY STARVE.' The Dean, while condemning it as inexcusable vandalism using anonymous and cowardly tactics, also noted that it was a message 'we cannot ignore'. Cathedrals and abbeys were the forerunners of the modern welfare state. They had always shown a lively concern for the poor and underprivileged.

He wrote: 'I believe we can complete Liverpool Cathedral with a clear conscience, for Christian inspiration still provides a momentum for much of the work undertaken by organizations and pressure groups for the relief of need in all parts of the world. . . .

'Yet the writing on the wall should give us all pause for thought, even if we disapprove of the way in which the message was conveyed. We have to be continually asking ourselves how this cathedral we are building for the worship of God can also be a powerhouse for compassion and concern. We hope that by preaching, drama, exhibitions, and in many other ways, that our duty to our brother is inextricably bound up with our duty to God.'

Another main point of contention was that less than a mile away the Roman Catholics had produced a cathedral for their archdiocese in just over four and a half years. Sir Frederick Gibberd's design was originally given a cost limit of £1 million, and when the cathedral was consecrated on 14 May 1967, the task could be regarded as completed. Admittedly, it was a building in reinforced concrete and in a completely different mode, but it could hold a large congregation and was extremely functional. It was a realistic end product from a Church which had originally planned to build the world's second largest cathedral in Liverpool, but which had taken note of the new post-war economic climate and had changed course.

The *New Christian*, a paper which Edward Patey regarded as the best of religious journals, carried an article, headed 'Liverpool Folly', about the Metropolitan Cathedral. It also had a swipe at Scott's edifice. The article said: 'The Anglican cathedral is a major problem for those who are required to use it and find funds for its ultimate completion', concluding: 'Their task seems likely to become even more difficult as the secular community moves further away from the medieval concepts which led to the planning of this building. . . . A pilgrim church cannot spend its time, thought, and money on monumental buildings. This is the day of the prefab rather than the baronial mansion, and it would be good to think that Britain's latest cathedral might also be its last.'

The reply came swiftly in Dean Patey's next newsletter: 'There is, I believe, no cathedral in the country which so adequately provides the flexibility and adaptability with its essential pre-requisite of modern community worship. . . .'

Liverpool Cathedral had been started in the grand manner. To stop now would be unthinkable. Yet as time went on, costs soared to a new high. The galloping inflation of the mid-seventies, which was defeating governments thoughout the Western World, was not to defeat the cathedral builders. The Nave and West Front was not just an ornament. It gave an extra dimension, an additional work area and theatre for experiment. As work progressed, the full glory of the building had been enhanced by the vista through the interior semi-circular bridge arch, which had been donated by the Dulverton Trust founded by Lord Dulverton, former chairman of the Imperial Tobacco Company.

But no matter how pleasing the effect, the final appeal for £460,000, launched in May 1976, was the most difficult yet from an ethical point of view. It was a job for a diplomat.

The Bishop, David Sheppard, who had arrived in Liverpool only the year before, was asked on a BBC local radio programme if the money could be better spent on the homeless. 'I agonize over the question myself,' he replied. 'If someone had suggested that we begin to build a mighty cathedral on this scale today, I would have no hesitation in voting against it.'

The real question, he said, was whether to honour the visionaries of the past. 'While I deeply believe that the Church is not called to spend huge sums on itself, I think it is right that we give priority to worshipping God and to proclaiming the greatness and glory of God. This is what this cathedral is trying to do,' he concluded.

The Dean also went on radio—to hold out the begging bowl. In a national appeal he said that to leave the work unfinished would make the cathedral builders 'the laughing stock of future generations'. The appeal chairman went further. He said it would be another failure in a city 'where things do not really happen at the moment'.

The Bishop added that the cathedral was a 'beacon of hope' for the inner city and the Lord Mayor asked everyone to 'keep faith with our ancestors'.

As the summit was approached, statements to justify the cathedral became more frenetic. The Dean lost no opportunity in telling the Press that the place was often filled to capacity. He published letters of support from far and wide. One person from Kent wrote: 'I remember writing to my father who was vicar of a parish in mid-Wales, that General Wolfe was quoted as saying that he would prefer being author of Gray's *Elegy* to the glory of beating the French at Quebec. I added that I would have preferred to have designed Liverpool Cathedral than either.'

One lady wrote: 'I don't expect we should agree on theology, but theology is only one of the many ways into the Kingdom of Heaven. I love the cathedral and I don't like to see an unfinished job. Only wish this was not the old maid's mite, but an old maid's thumping donation.'

There was the Liverpool letter which read: 'I am enclosing my savings with a prayer that in God's own time everything that is needed will come along', and the anonymous donation from 'a pauper who more than once has been entranced and inspired by the beauty of that magnificent building'. Another letter was from a Birkenhead schoolgirl who enclosed her pocket money.

But all this did not stop dissension within the ranks of the Church. One local vicar, using his parish magazine as a vehicle for his feelings, demanded to know why estimates on

10 The cathedral tower, floodlit.

the earlier appeal had fallen so short, and continued: 'The money would be better spent on the parishes which are desperately hard up. . . .'

Yet the generosity of the public—the fortunes of merchant princes and the mites of widows—knocked all the critics into touch. Nobody ever gave a penny to Liverpool Cathedral under duress. No matter what their inner motives—even boastfulness, pride, or vanity—they gave because they wanted to. Under those circumstances, one may even begin to ask whether all the hard work of justification to satisfy the anti-cathedral lobby, was really required. At the end of the day a useful cost perspective is provided by the fact that in 1977 British television companies spent £14 million on religious spectaculars—enough to build a score of Gothic cathedrals at medieval prices.

And so Liverpool completed its glorious cathedral. The people of the diocese had not set out to build the largest church in Britain. It had evolved from a concept initiated by Bishop Chavasse who wanted accommodation for at least 3,000 people within easy hearing distance of the preacher. That building has now been brought to fruition. It has been made to last for a thousand years.

5

Cathedral Community

> The cathedral is itself a kind of city, a more meta-
> physical one than the physical city outside, yet as
> complicated, diverse, and multifold in its functions
> and spaces.
>
> PATRICK NUTTGENS

'Good morning, the cathedral.' It is 9 am and in the general office Stanley Williams is taking his first telephone call of the day. Somebody visiting Merseyside from Sussex wants to know the times of services. A few minutes later, another caller is asking whether the Western Rooms can be booked for a conference. And so it goes on: people wanting to send cheques for building maintenance; a student who wants to know the Dean's initials; a woman who hopes she will be able to confirm to a friend that the place really is bigger than York Minster; a young man who wants to speak to a member of the Chapter because his marriage is breaking up.

Stanley has worked here for all three deans. He started off as a verger before becoming cathedral Secretary. With him in the office is Geoffrey Rimmer, a cathedral chorister who went to art school, was asked to help out at the cathedral, and has worked here ever since. This particular morning he is typing and duplicating service sheets for Sunday. Stanley has already telephoned a local schoolmistress to ask if she will read the epistle. She accepts, and because she is already familiar with speaking in the cathedral's difficult acoustics, no rehearsal will be necessary.

The cathedral has been open since 8.30 am. That is when Bill Blundell, the maintenance engineer, arrived. His first job today is to fix some lighting in the Ambulatory.

In his own office, the Chancellor, Basil Naylor, is letter-writing. One reply which particularly pleases him is to a student who remembers an article he wrote on the theological aspects of Bach's chorales. Then the processional order and seating arrangements for a big service have to be sorted out. The afternoon will see him hospital-visiting.

The Dean is putting the finishing touches to his latest book, which has to be at the publisher's in a couple of days. He has already dictated the last chapter on tape, but is reading through the typescript of an earlier one. He has been through the mail, sent off some replies. There is the installation of an honorary canon to be set up and a speech to be written for a church conference in the Midlands. The early morning staff meeting had covered a lot of ground and some of the items would be raised at the Chapter Meeting next month. There is a lunch appointment at the cathedral today with a visiting American preacher.

Tourist parties have been arriving at the cathedral in a steady flow since about 9.30 am. The first is a group of German students, who will be taken around by one of the cathedral interpreters (the name given to guides who are also asked to interpret the role of the building). The day's schedule includes a class of local schoolchildren and a women's guild from Cheshire. All these are in addition to the couple of hundred visitors—families, friends, and individuals—who will wander about on their own or latch on to a larger party being given a conducted tour.

The bookstall run by Bunny Hunter, president and founder member of the Cross Guild (former choristers), is doing good business selling illustrated guidebooks, colour slides, key rings, and records of the cathedral choir and organ.

In the main body of the building, the head verger, Len Collins, is supervising the 'turn-round' of seating following a concert the previous evening. All the chairs had been facing a platform in the Central Space; now they must face the High Altar for Saturday's Sung Evensong. Not so many seats will be needed, so some can be stacked up, put on the floor lift, and stored in the basement.

Cleaners are busy brushing the side aisles of the Choir; some children are told by one of the vergers not to play 'tick' in the Central Space, while by the Nave Bridge, members of the German party are paying for a trip to the top of the tower. In the Western Transept a local charity organization is setting up a photographic exhibition.

The sound of organ music can be heard. In the Lady Chapel, the cathedral organist, Noel Rawsthorne, is running through some items for a recital the following week. The music adds to the enjoyment of visitors, who seek it out and sit listening while looking at the architecture around them.

Back in the office, Deaconess Thelma Tomlinson is telling a curate about the success of her latest play scheme. This is when children from the neighbourhood take to the Chapter House to paint and draw, make cut-outs, and design murals. It helps them fight off the boredom of school holidays.

By now Geoffrey Rimmer is addressing envelopes to be sent to the printer of the cathedral music list. From there the service details will be mailed to people all over the country.

The Canon Precentor, Gordon Bates, is fixing up details for a group of Renaissance singers who want to perform in the Lady Chapel as part of a North-West tour. Later he is to see some ordinands whom he is responsible for, and to hold a meeting with choirboys' parents.

At the same time Leslie Hopkins, the Canon Treasurer, has agreed to take on some casual staff as holiday relief. They will stand in for the vergers as required. Final details of a Mothers' Union service will need to be planned after lunch.

Down in the Undercroft the Dean's meal is cooking: roast beef and Yorkshire pudding. Across the way, in the music library, Bill Dale, one of the cathedral's voluntary helpers, is binding copies of an anthem for the choir.

The Dean's visitor arrives. The American has never been here before. He is amazed at the scale and grandeur of the place—far bigger than it looks in photographs. But there are the more intimate areas too, like the Chapel of the Holy Spirit, designed for prayer and meditation. At this moment, a middle-aged woman sits alone with her thoughts.

After lunch one of the Cross Guild boys who have been operating the tower lift comes to the office for change. That morning they have taken £13. Just then, a man in shabby clothing comes in and asks for the boat fare to Dublin. He is told to see one of the clergy who puts him in touch with the Social Services who may be able to assist.

The Dean's visitor has left and the Dean returns to answer some more letters, speaks at length on the telephone to a member of the Community Relations Council, and gives an interview to a journalist writing about experiments in worship.

Len Collins has already made preparations for Evensong. It will be a 'said' service in the Lady Chapel.

Just after 4 pm the choirboys arrive from school for practice. Pop and cakes have been prepared for them. The Director of Music, Ronald Wean, himself a schoolmaster, puts them through their paces in the Song Room of the Undercroft. Earlier, some of the boys' cassocks had been sewn and repaired by a group of lady helpers.

By 5 pm things are beginning to wind down. The office closes, the visitors thin out, the vergers make their final rounds before lock-up. Only Len Collins remains to open the Western Rooms in the evening for a meeting of probation officers. Other members of the cathedral family are ready to go home. . . .

Extracts and impressions of another typical day of activity. It has been an ordinary day without any of the great services and processions which characterize cathedral life to most people; a working day in which people have got on with the graft of administration, ministry, pastoral care, maintaining musical standards, and money raising.

And for those who have visited Liverpool Cathedral for the first time, it has been a very special day. They have seen an architectural showpiece, and perhaps much more. They may have noticed that they became part of a community within the community, where mission is the fundamental principle.

Canon Roger Lloyd, the late Vice-Dean of Winchester, wrote in his book *The Church of England 1900–65*: 'To fail to be a community is to fail at the point at which cathedrals have often been vulnerable and sometimes still are. This failure, where it exists, is the more devastating in that it seriously detracts from the fulfilling of any other ministry.'

Lloyd rightly believed that cathedrals were themselves communities which could lead the Church's advance into the modern age. Responsibilities for pioneering the breakthrough lay with them. 'Who else can do it?' he asked in a letter to *The Times*. 'The central administration of the Church is smothering all possibility of prophetic leadership by the weight of its own paperwork. The bishops struggle against it, but the diocesan administrative machinery, being tied to Dean's Yard, had no choice but to follow its methods with the same results.

'But cathedrals are independent. Most of them are alert and alive and full of activity.

'Deans and Chapters have long ceased to be nests of jealousy and intrigue. A team ministry is perfectly possible for them, and in many cathedrals is now being carried on.'

Liverpool Cathedral Chapter feel that they can legitimately claim to be sharing in that pioneering spirit. Their ministry is not hindered by notions of what is 'proper' in a cathedral. Yet while its role today is very different from that envisaged at the beginning of the century, there is still every need to gather support for what happens within the building. As Dean Patey has said: 'Our work will be of little value unless we carry with us the confidence of the clergy of the diocese. We exist to be of service to them as they work in the front line of the ministry in their parishes.'

This did not mean conservatism. There would obviously be a 'risk' element if new ground was to be broken. Back in 1966 Dean Patey had declared: 'This is an age which demands a reappraisal of our traditional religious ways of thinking, of our age-old pattern of worship, and of our strategy in the community. Only a dead church will not be profoundly influenced by these changes. The continual decline in church attendances suggests that those changes have not yet been considered seriously enough.'

Historically, cathedrals had come to be regarded as unchanging, insular bodies, inhabited by the clever and the rich, for the giving out of advice and charity to the less clever and the poor. Their physical insularity had grown from the monastic conception of a church surrounded by refectory, cloister and infirmary, or choir school, library, and clergy residences. The need gradually changed to require buildings which fitted into the ordinary pattern of everyday life.

It has been said that cathedrals exist *ad majorem Dei gloriam*, and that a community feeling is not the most important aspect: that they were made to outspan the coming and going of the generations. But such an argument is destined to failure in today's world, where the Church, like all establishment bodies, is battling with a tidal wave of scepticism and dissent.

However, it is curious to note that Liverpool Cathedral belongs to one of the great ages of cathedral building. America, Asia, and Africa have all erected or planned new cathedrals during the time of Liverpool's building, as have three dioceses in this country. Is this the last outbreak of madness in a materialistic and ungodly world, or a signal for new hope in the future?

The consecration of Coventry Cathedral in 1962 brought a new surge of interest in cathedral life. So did the completion of Liverpool's Metropolitan Cathedral five years later. The Anglican cathedral now poses these questions afresh and probably more pointedly than ever before. The fact that new and exciting things have already been happening here for three generations is irrelevant to the currency which the completion has given to the issues.

The cathedrals have become Liverpool's major tourist attractions, but the Churches—Anglican and Roman—see them as much more. They are living and on-going communities. Dean Patey says, with typical use of imagery: 'Liverpool is proud of itself as a swinging city. To many people this means football and the Mersey Sound of the sixties. But we can be certain that long after the football craze has given way to something else and the Mersey Sound forgotten, Liverpool will be known as the city of two cathedrals, and people will look back in wonder at this twentieth century when men had the vision to build two such great manifestations of their faith in God.'

When Coventry Cathedral opened, Dean Dillistone saluted the vast number of people who produced a great work of art. 'Is it not this fact which is mainly responsible for the abiding significance of a cathedral church, not only in ecclesiastical circles, but also in the general life of a nation?' he asked. 'Through it a community belonging to a city, perhaps to a particular geographical area, seeks to offer its best to God through a fusion within a composite whole of the finest products of every department of its common life.'

The new age of cathedral building also provided a fresh impetus for self-criticism. Where other Chapters had inherited long-standing traditions, the twentieth-century cathedrals had the opportunity of beginning their history amid a far greater feeling of expectancy.

At the time of Liverpool Cathedral's consecration, the Cathedrals Commission had not begun its work. The cathedrals of ancient status seemed to be dominated by establishment custom, so weighed down with statutory obligations as to be hardly capable of a fresh start. They were not easily moved from their routine. Those of the later dioceses were almost all parish churches with a long history behind them. Neither could face the situation *de novo*. It was a case of amending an ancient script rather than starting with a clean sheet. All these truths were being recognized against a background of black statistics, which indicated that cathedrals as communities were losing ground.

Canon John Hunter, adviser in mission to the Archbishop of York, reported in a working paper on unity, theology, and mission to northern church leaders that Western Christian churches had suffered 'not only a massive haemorrhage of support, but also a loss of morale which has proved debilitating to their task of speaking to society in a meaningful and prophetic way'.

The missionary basis of the Church was being eroded by growing unbelief and scepticism, said Canon Hunter, who is also an honorary canon of Liverpool Cathedral. Churches had begun to take a joint look at mission because of the spectre of eventual oblivion, he suggested.

In the fifteenth and sixteenth centuries there had been a growth of public support. The nineteenth century also brought renewed interest and a new rash of denominations. But the great evangelical campaigns of this century had made little or no difference to the steady drift from the churches.

Cathedral communities looked as if they might become impotent within the life of the dioceses. Stuart Blanch, when Bishop of Liverpool, had produced a document for group consultation which said: 'One of the felt needs of twentieth-century England is the sense of meaninglessness or loss of personal identity caused by the progressive enlargement of political and economic structures, and by the palpable absence of any generally accepted direction in which to steer national or individual life.'

While groups of churches in the Call to the North missionary campaign of the sixties had occasionally produced spectacular one-off results (not least in the 'Orange and Green' area of Liverpool's Everton district) many cathedrals still had a lot of ground to make up in showing themselves to be relevant and credible. They were being forced to learn all over again that people and community awareness mattered more than buildings; that the Church is human beings, not bricks, mortar, and stone.

This was certainly the case at Liverpool Cathedral, when the 1968 Finish the Cathedral appeal was launched. Edward Patey had said: 'We must never become slaves to plant and machinery. Since the Church exists primarily for others and not for itself, it must be more concerned with the service it renders to the world than with its own well-being and survival.'

The Dean had touched the very nerve which made so many people opposed to cathedral appeals. They felt that such exercises detracted from the root evangelism and service which was the real calling of Christianity. The priority had to be given to grass-roots parish ministry. They proclaimed that the future lay with smaller community groups meeting in houses, offices, factories, and schools, and with common action at these centres of 'real life'.

If cathedrals were to survive and find a place in everyday society, radical redefinition of their purpose was necessary. Any affirmation of faith in their community role was therefore more welcome when it came from outside the ranks of the Church. This 'common touch' was free from any counter-gibes about self defence from within the ministry.

At a service for European Architectural Heritage Year at Liverpool Cathedral, Patrick Nuttgens, director of Leeds Polytechnic, came up with the goods. He said that cathedrals were not just places for worship. They were 'meeting places' and a symbol of unity. 'The cathedral is itself a kind of city, a more metaphysical one than the physical city outside, yet as complicated, diverse, and multifold in its functions and spaces,' said Dr Nuttgens.

Such statements were always warmly applauded by clerics who saw themselves as in danger of losing the battle for a place in people's minds. But scholarly words and verbal definition were not enough.

Liverpool Cathedral, while facing the same problems as all cathedrals, had managed to ride the storm. And while it had established its own community, it also strove to speak to the larger community of Merseyside through its actions. Tailor-made services, experimentation, bold—even controversial—attitudes and confrontations had helped to keep the elements of worship as active as the elements of building and money-raising during its formative years. Perhaps successive Chapters can claim to have found the difference between religion and community mission: locally, nationally, and inter-nationally.

Recent years have seen important links established with Washington Cathedral (still under construction); Trondheim Cathedral (the 'Westminster Abbey' of Norway); and particularly Namirembe Cathedral, the chief provincial church of Uganda.

In 1972 the Dean of Namirembe, Yokana Mukasa (now Bishop of Mityana) stayed in Liverpool as a guest of the cathedral Chapter, sharing in their day-to-day activities. Since then the Chancellor, Canon Basil Naylor, has been to

Namirembe, but was prevented from carrying out a survey for the Christian Organizations Research and Advisory Trust, because of the political situation. And in 1976, Michael Kalule, musical director at Namirembe, came to England for a three-month course at the Royal School of Church Music. Liverpool Cathedral contributed to the costs and has also sent a considerable amount of printed choral music to Namirembe, where the economic climate makes the provision of sheet music virtually impossible.

'It's difficult to maintain this particular link today,' says Basil Naylor, 'because we have to be careful not to endanger our friends in corresponding with them. We feel very much involved in their plight, and I know from communications which have come to me in a roundabout way—of necessity— how much they value our friendship.'

So once again Liverpool Cathedral finds itself at the front line of Christian concern, with all the world as its stage.

6

Worshipful Ways

> You have to go to Liverpool Cathedral if you want
> to see how to walk to the glory of God. Every pro-
> cession is an act of worship.
>
> CLIFFORD MARTIN

The cathedral's Central Space had been transformed into a
fairground. Coloured lights flashed on and off and the smell
of incense filled every corner. Youngsters blew soap bubbles
and carried balloons on sticks. Others listened to a folk
group beneath the Nave bridge. At the West a film was being
shown. Some teenagers browsed around the many bookstalls
on which they found material about the underprivileged, the
homeless, the illiterate, and the persecuted.

Small discussion groups had been organized to talk over
such issues. On the steps of the Choir, members of a large
impromptu gathering were arguing about the meaning of
evangelism. The new communion service setting was being
analysed by students in the War Memorial Chapel. The
sound of guitars gave way to the swell of an organ improvization. There was singing and dancing. In the Lady Chapel
three short Bach organ recitals were complemented by
periods of spontaneous prayer.

As dawn began to break, Bishop Trevor Huddleston,
visiting from Stepney, inspired the thousand-strong gathering with a personal devotion to Christ, after which he and the
Dean led in an act of sharing in which loaves of bread were
broken and distributed to everyone.

So began one of the most unusual ecumenical youth
conferences in recent years. Yet not everyone who popped
into the cathedral on that August night in 1973 professed
to be Christian. They didn't have to be. Liverpool was
providing an 'Operation Welcome' to both strangers and
pilgrims from all over Britain. Those who had thought of the
primary aim of the Church as being to prepare people for

death, were being given a salutary lesson: this event was concerned with life together in the present.

Edward Patey was jubilant about the result: 'It spoke to me more eloquently about the relationship between worship, celebration, community, and caring than any other event in which I have been involved. If anyone ever asks whether it is necessary to have such a building, they should have come into the cathedral on that night. I believe we have a central meeting space which is second to none in the world.'

There was encouragement from other denominations. Dr Kenneth Slack, Moderator of the General Assembly of the United Reformed Church, told a Festival of Friends service at Norwich Cathedral that same year: 'If the cathedral is the place where the norm of Anglican worship should find its loveliest and most enriched expression, it is also the place where carefully planned, yet courageous and imaginative experiments in worship ought to take place, and where worship must be devised to meet the needs and express the inspirations of the most varied companies.'

Not everyone held such views. People could be relied upon to complain in the most vitriolic manner. In this instance most of the protests came from within the diocese, where the majority of the publicity for the youth rally was centred.

But television brought greater risks. Few events in the history of the cathedral have led to so much discussion as the 1967 Christmas Eve transmission called 'How on Earth?'. Undertaken by ATV, it featured one of the top pop groups of the day, The Bee Gees and folk music (including songs from The Crofters, all former Liverpool Cathedral choristers). It had disc jockey Kenny Everett reading the Gospel in Scouse, and drama from the Liverpool Everyman Theatre Company. It showed teenage girls dancing and screaming in front of their idols, and embracing their boyfriends. There were also unofficial reports of smoking and beer drinking.

The response couldn't have been louder had the cathedral roof fallen in. The Dean's postbag made interesting reading.

From Cheshire: 'Disgusted, disgusted, disgusted. To think of a most beautiful cathedral brought down to these depths—

11 The showbiz Dean: Edward Patey tries his hand as a drummer with the Bee Gees.

a programme suitable for the Cavern Club and other similar places.'

A Hampshire correspondent wrote: 'We feel compelled to protest about the broadcast from your cathedral, watched by millions. Quite apart from the whole gimmick of the programme, we felt deeply ashamed at the unnecessarily crude and vulgar form of the presentation that could have brought enlightenment about the significance of the Christmas story to no one, and could only have offended those to whom it meant everything. We tried in vain to discover the real motive that lay behind this travesty.'

A Merseyside church organist complained: 'I refer to the disgusting beat group that was allowed to enter our homes. I thought I was on the wrong programme until I saw these terrible faces and low-down entertainment focused in the sacred pillars of a Christian place of worship. Many friends of mine, including my own choir, feel very strongly about this and demand some sort of explanation.'

From Hertfordshire: 'Do you realize that by allowing this programme to be shown you have contributed towards accelerating the decline of Christianity and the Church in general? It was in extremely bad taste, quite apart from the effect it may have had on any children who were watching. Need anyone remind you that the Church is not a disco-theque, cinema, or night club?'

And from London: 'I felt thoroughly upset and ashamed. To me the beautiful story of Christ's birth was made a mockery of. I hope that we shall never again witness a performance which so cheapened God's house and religion.'

Fortunately for the Dean, letters of approval outnumbered the complaints. An Oxford theologian said: 'The impact of the spoken words was highly dramatic and surely effective. It was grand to see the cathedral seething with young people.'

An American visitor advised: 'Because I know that you will receive some severe criticism, perhaps I can help you to override it a bit. I am now living in London with my three children. Through a series of tragic circumstances, we have become estranged from the Church . . . an estrange-ment which was partly healed by your programme.'

From a churchwoman and playwright: 'I wanted to ring you up straight away, but guessed that you would be far too busy for telephone calls. Of its kind it is the best I have ever seen, and I must congratulate you and the producers for the way in which you used the cathedral.'

A Sussex viewer concluded: 'Simply wonderful. I am over sixty, but feel that if more churches had what you gave, they would attract more young people.'

The local and national Press were also for the Dean. The *Liverpool Daily Post* reporter said: 'I could find little to criticize on the grounds of irreverence. The huge crowd of youngsters seemed very attentive most of the time.'

The *Daily Mirror* said: 'It was a knock-out. The kids took the House of God by storm. Call this mixture of secular and sacred "Beat the Devil" if you like, but it certainly packed the church. It expressed as no other programme did, the spirit of Christmas. Praise the Lord and pass the Bee Gees.'

The *Sun* said that Kenny Everett told the Christmas story 'in simple, straightforward terms that held his teenage audience—and all of us'.

The Dean produced a special report on the event. 'Church-going girls are as susceptible to pop hysteria as anyone else, and this produced certain problems. On the other hand, the Church must learn to use the talents which people have, and I believe that, on balance, the introduction of the pop group was justified.'

The event was a 'production' designed for a mass audience and, in television terms, took its place alongside Midnight Eucharist from Manchester Cathedral, a carol service from King's College, Cambridge, and a performance of Bach's *Christmas Oratorio*.

At the cathedral it had been planned in conjunction with two traditional carol services, a recital by the choir, motets from the Renaissance Music Group, and the staging of the fifteenth-century Wakefield Miracle Plays by the Everyman Company.

Without such a programme, both cathedral and television would have ignored a considerable section of the community in their Christmas presentations. This should have given a splendid opportunity of making the missionary point that the Church is the only society which exists for the benefit of those who do not belong to it. Unfortunately, some people, including some clergy, did not see this and a certain amount of disorder resulted.

The Church could not be tied to one cultural pattern, said the Dean. And it had been cultural rather than theological grounds which had resulted in most of the shock and anger. Nevertheless, the programme had proved to be a litmus paper for public reaction to the use of cathedrals and what should be allowed to happen in a church building.

The following year, J. G. Davies, Professor of Theology at Birmingham University, had this to say in his book *The Secular Use of Church Buildings*: 'How is a consecrated building to be defined? Negatively, it is not to be defined as a habitation of God, nor a shrine of the Divine presence. It is not the modern counterpart of the Jerusalem Temple. Nor is it a holy place in that it has a character of "wholly otherness" set apart from the world.

'In so far as the word "holy" can be used at all, this must be understood functionally to mean "God-relatedness". A consecrated building is therefore one in which the secular is God-related explicitly and the unit of life is thereby shown forth.

'In the past a church has always been understood functionally, but this function has been restricted to worship conceived solely as a cultic activity. . . . Our argument leads to the affirmation that either it is wrong to limit the meaning of worship in this way, or that it is necessary to acknowledge that the function of a church building is more complex than has previously been conceived. Its function is to serve the mission of God. . . . It must therefore minister to human need and at the same time its explicit God-relatedness declares the unity of all in Christ.'

The sentiments were ideally those of the Dean of Liverpool, who was to stretch the definition to its extreme in 1975 by sanctioning a concert by the German group, Tangerine Dream. Synthesized quadrophonic sound complemented the 'God-relatedness' of the building. 'In their wordless improvization, there is layer upon layer of built-up sound, which will be matched architecturally in the pillars, vaulting, and arches,' he promised. 'Today in art, as in morals, politics, and much else, we easily become divided and polarized. The Christian faith is concerned with reconciliation and the breaking down of barriers.'

In more general terms the Dean was to say in a lecture at the St Nicholas Church Museum, Bristol, in October 1976: 'Even those who have come to Liverpool Cathedral who have no particular religious conviction or faith, to proclaim their often Marxist-biased views through poetry and song, concede that this building gives a new dimension to what they are doing.'

The often outrageous medieval mystery plays testify to the once good relationship between the Church and popular art. The Church has always attracted creative minds: the cantatas

12 Moving the seating round and using the backcloth provided by the Nave Bridge, turns the cathedral into a concert hall for a great choral occasion.

of Bach; the altarpieces by Rubens and Titian; the mosaics of Ravenna, and so on. Yet today, despite Eliot's *Murder in the Cathedral* (commissioned by the Friends of Canterbury Cathedral) and Benjamin Britten's *War Requiem*, written for the opening of Coventry Cathedral, art is no longer in the mainstream of church offering and worship, said the Dean.

When Dean Patey preached at the dedication of the South Transept of the still incomplete Washington Cathedral in 1971, he told his American congregation: 'Christians themselves are sometimes more interested in clinging to the *status quo* than reaching out into the future in response to that God who is always on the side of what is coming into being. And the search for that dynamic God, at times, seems to be pursued with greater expectation, integrity, and imagination in the world of technology and drama, art and politics and social involvement than in the seemingly tired institution we call the Church.'

Liverpool has increasingly tried to revive interest in a Renaissance of arts in worship. As Professor Davies, already quoted in this chapter, has pointed out: 'It would not be an exaggeration to say that dance is the human activity *par excellence* which mostly corresponds to the Christian doctrine of the incarnation, and as such could be regarded as a necessary element in the worship of the incarnate, crucified, and resurrected God.'

Dance has already been used in moderation at the cathedral. Drama has found a greater role, but the Dean wishes to expand both fields. Great choral works, including two performances of Mahler's *Symphony of a Thousand*, directed by Sir Charles Groves, have gained immeasurably from the atmosphere of the building.

At an anniversary organ recital Noel Rawsthorne played Liverpool composer John McCabe's Eastertide work *Dies Resurrectiones*, while lighting effects were focused on panels of the High Altar reredos and relevant passages of Scripture were read between movements.

All these recitals, concerts, plays, dance works, folk and pop dates are seen by the Chapter as essential to the cathedral's role as a centre for worship, and not as optional extras for an élitist audience. 'They are all acts which acknowledge that God is the source of all creativity,' says Dean Patey.

If the overtly spectacular or experimental has created most interest in recent years, it is merely a reflection of the items which tend to interest the media. Yet two other aspects of what Professor Davies calls God-relatedness—the liturgical and the communal—have had a no less interesting history at Liverpool. Indeed, they reflect a story of how the once experimental has now become the traditional.

The cathedral had in its first Dean a man with a rare genius for the ordering of worship. He gave services a dignity and relevance which earned him a worldwide reputation. Frederick Dwelly had infinite resource, imagination, sympathy, and institutional sensitivity. The Press was to praise him for the 'aesthetic architecture' he placed within the physical architecture of his emerging building. If Scott had been the brain behind the material cathedral, Dwelly was surely the father of its spiritualism.

When the building was about to be consecrated, Bishop Augustus David had told Canon Charles Raven (later to be Chancellor) that he did not know how to devise a service worthy of the occasion. Raven had spent the first four days of Holy Week at Emmanuel Church, Southport where Dwelly was vicar. On the last evening they had sat up together until after midnight, planning the Easter service. When Raven went to bed, the script was a mass of corrections, yet the same script appeared in print ready for distribution when his morning tea arrived.

In the early hours Dwelly had cycled to see his friend, the foreman printer of the local newspaper, and asked him to send up the printed form with the milk! The parish of Emmanuel certainly had a man of action at the helm, and when Raven told the Bishop this story, and of Dwelly's knowledge of the liturgy and church music, he was asked to 'produce' the cathedral's consecration service.

'Dwelly rose at once to the occasion, set chairs for the royal visitors in the King's Porch and carried through the whole programme without a sign of anxiety,' Raven reported.

It was this precision and artistic eye for what made a great service that earned the cathedral processions the nickname of 'Dwelly's Circus'. Yet no man was better suited to hold the office of first Dean when the Chapter was set up in 1931. Today he is remembered as a 'benevolent autocrat' who was the guiding light of the Liverpool tradition. He would change the choice of hymns during a service, ask for music to be stopped in mid-flow if it suited the 'shape' of the event, alter schedules and details at the eleventh hour, and ask the choir to return to practise moving in procession through the building.

If there is any objective criticism to be made about the Dwelly period, it was that the cathedral atmosphere became rather too aloof during the later years when the Dean was in ill health. Earlier on, there had been some friction between the Dean and Bishop David, who is reported to have been reluctant to let go of some of the responsibilities he had had before the cathedral Chapter was formed. Those who could see the tensions developing even planned an evening of reconciliation over a meal at Liverpool's Adelphi Hotel. One observer caught the spirit of the evening by referring to the mood as one of 'an olive branch floating in champagne'. Later, it was probably Dwelly's illness and increasing vagueness which caused a rift with some of the local churches. The Chancellor, Canon Basil Naylor, sums up: 'I think the cathedral company tended to think of themselves as a separate section away from the diocese. There was a tendency to become rather like a Vatican chapel rather than the mother church of the area.'

But not even these developments can diminish Dwelly's ultimate stature in the cathedral's history and his contribution to the order of its worship and founding of its traditions. 'Although he was no longer here when I arrived, I could sense his presence,' says Canon Naylor. 'Everyone from the Cross Guild to the cleaners were still hung around Dwelly. They had the tradition almost built into them.'

Bishop Clifford Martin said when Dwelly retired in 1955: 'You have to go to Liverpool Cathedral if you want to see how to walk to the glory of God. Every procession is an act of worship.'

Dwelly was an autocrat who took an immense interest in what everyone was doing. Even the smallest boy in the choir was made to think of himself as an important factor in the common act of praise and prayer.

For the consecration it was evident that no repetition of a traditional service would suffice. Neither would a collection of ancient ceremonies and formulae combined into an office. What was needed was a service which while fulfilling all that past experience could suggest, should possess a coherence, a rhythm, and an appropriateness of its own for the circumstances of the day. Dwelly and his Chapter believed that as worship should be man's supreme activity and joy, repetition was an insult to the purpose of the cathedral. At the same time they began a tight-rope walk (which has always continued) in weaving together the heritage of yesterday with the promise and challenge of tomorrow.

Two of Dwelly's chancellors, Charles Raven and J. S. Bezzant, were modernists, which gave added colour to the older kind of liberalism that was quite strong in the cathedral at the time.

In a bygone age, worship had been the characteristic activity of the community. The liturgical offerings associated with Plough Sunday, Rogation Sunday, and so on, reflected the rhythm of work in which everyone was involved. Familiar faces from the workaday world were portrayed in the corbels of churches or under the miserere seats in the choir. Commerce was linked with the parish churches through the ancient fairs which centred on the patronal festivals. Churches responsible for pioneer acts of charity became the forerunners of the modern welfare state. Almshouses, grammar schools, and colleges dedicated to 'godliness and good learning' were also attached to the churches. But in the second quarter of the twentieth century, churches and cathedrals were making ever less impact on the community. Local government hardly recognized their existence. Unless a new approach was found, that division would widen. The rule was to advance with caution.

Those members of the cathedral staff who were there in the formative years often quote Dean Dwelly's famous reply to those who were perhaps too eager to shelve the past. 'What you are proposing may be all right with Dr Dwelly, but the first Dean of Liverpool has to be careful, because what he allows will stand as precedents for all time.'

Edward Patey—despite his sense of adventure—still holds fast to the Dwelly principle: 'A cathedral, by its status, and by the fact that deans are put into office by royal appointment, is one of the mother churches of the nation. There will always be this tension between the past and the future. We cannot wave goodbye to the past and we cannot fail to proclaim the church of the future.'

Charles Raven, writing about the early years at Liverpool, said: 'To the sceptical, there is ample room for disbelief. The whole achievement may seem no more than a dramatic performance, an individual preciosity. Such critics must recognize that to many, the services in Liverpool Cathedral have opened up a new apprehension of the eternal and a new outlook upon life; that visitors come from all quarters and all classes, and that they are gradually convincing the Church that here is a new avenue for their work, a new means of conveying the experience of God to the souls of men.'

Dwelly believed that the most important function of his cathedral was 'to manifest towards God the Church's acknowledgement of dependence upon his creative generosity'. The words must therefore be well considered. They must also be formal, corporate in sense, and responsive in significance. He would often use the words of Archbishop Lang that a cathedral 'should give continuous witness to the things unseen and eternal and to offer continuous and reverent worship'.

Dwelly had particular faith in services which are subsidiary to the normal liturgical offices, since the demands of the day were bound to strain the limits of strictly regulated liturgy. He called these 'liturgical services for non-liturgical people'.

The layman's potential contribution, he considered, was great. He once wrote at considerable length on the subject. 'The method of gathering is simple. It is certainly direct. The evangelists would surely discern in it a true way of evangelism. It has a genuine touch of the primitive about it.

'But although the method is simple, it is never easy. It has no publicity value, for it permits no shred of insincerity. It certainly brings a profoundly deep spiritual experience to the conductor. The offerings of divine acknowledgement that laymen have taken immense trouble over, in an attempt to present it worthily, move me deeply.

' . . . It is the preparation of the prayers and responses with laymen that matters. This inspiration derived from laymen is the key of a new evangelism, a personal soul-winning, of seeking one by one in vocation after vocation. In such work is the very primitiveness of simplicity and the utterance of sincerity.

'It sacrifices all mere cataloguing of beautiful and devotional phrases of experiences that are unknown and emotions that are unfelt. It is from these acknowledgements, oblations, praises, and benedictions arising out of the actual experiences of the children of men, that there has come the new form of evangelization which gives birth to new acts of worship. ... At a critical point in the discussions, the laymen who are building Liverpool Cathedral threw their influence in a positive direction. By a resolution they prayed the Dean and Chapter to concentrate upon divine worship and on supplementary people's services as the principal works of the cathedral. The same laymen have untiringly sought out and presented for offering and worship the permanent values to be found in their several vocations. ... My experience convinces me that the non-liturgically minded are more easily to be led to the supremest acts of worship and communion if they are initiated through supplementary services. They have none of the thrill and none of the emotion of the crowded mass-missions—and none of their dangers.'

Dwelly was writing with a wealth of experience behind him in the doss-houses of London; in the Lake District countryside; in an educational centre in Gloucestershire; and in a Lancashire parish. Now this process of the Church translating itself out of the language and idioms of the traditional into the language and idioms of the real world, was paying dividends at Liverpool Cathedral. The 'People's Services' at 8.30 on Sunday evenings pulled capacity congregations, and although the cathedral was smaller in those days, the crowd regularly ran to more than four figures.

The Dwelly formula won wide praise. In a glowing end-of-war address in 1945, the Archbishop of York, Cyril Garbett, said: 'Your services hold a place of their own in the Anglican communion. The prayers and praises used are both old and new; the worship of the historic liturgies is combined with prayers for modern needs in present-day prose. And the appeal is made to the eye as well as to the ear, and to the imagination as well as to the intellect.

'Your services have thus become popular in the best sense of the word. They have significance not merely to a small group of the faithful who have been brought up to appreciate the ordinary worship of the Church, but to the people of a great city.

'Men of different professions and interests find in the special services of the cathedral, worship which is relevant to their daily work and problems.

'The wide spaces within it for prayer and contemplation should make them eager to provide without, spaces for peace and quiet for tired men and women and for the play of little children. The colour and glory within it should encourage attempts to bring more colour, variety, and interest into the lives which are spent in drab and dreary streets.'

Dwelly believed that the existence of the cathedral could not be justified if it were to minister only to people who left their parish churches to attend. He was out to capture the imagination and interest of the broadest cross-section of the public. From the day of his appointment, he lived in and worked for the cathedral, discovering new opportunities for its mission.

There has always been uncertainty within the Church over how mission should be approached. In the 1970s even the admirers of the mass evangelical movement are beginning to wonder whether this mission has had its day. Certainly the power of the pulpit is dwindling and the old kind of parochial mission is making less impact.

In the non-Roman Catholic world the message of mission has so often been based on the mission of Wesley and Whitfield two centuries ago. As Canon John Hunter, adviser in mission to the Archbishop of York, has pointed out: 'Wherever one turns in the sphere of mission, the prime concern is about method rather than message. No sooner is the idea of mission mooted in church circles than discussion immediately centres on how it should be accomplished.'

At Liverpool Cathedral there has always been the realization that mission cannot be left to the individual acting in isolation. Neither could it be dependent upon a small group acting sporadically in the hope of influencing its local culture. 'Mission today needs common witness, not only by the leadership, but at the same time by the laity,' says Hunter. The idea of such mission through worship has never been ignored at Liverpool. As the theologian Emil Brunner once said: 'The Church exists for mission as fire exists for burning.'

A host of special services have been devised since Dwelly's day to bridge the gaps and exploit the lay-potential of Merseyside. In recent times these have centred on civic life; the Forces; the consular service; the educational, legal, and medical professions; the arts, industry, and commerce; youth and children—and even a service in praise of World Cup soccer.

Chancellor Basil Naylor says: 'More and more groups are seeking to express themselves in a larger area than the normal city and urban life. A cathedral is mother, servant, and teacher, and our services reflect community interests.

'It was here that Dwelly achieved so much by breaking away from simply using the old prayer-book formulae. When services are suggested, we ask the people concerned what they want to say, and tailor the proceedings accordingly.'

An act of worship which combined ecumenism with social concern was one for the care of the offender. The sermon was given by Augustine Harris, Auxiliary Roman Catholic Bishop of Liverpool, and during the proceedings statements were given from two prisoners, a probation officer, the warden of a hostel for ex-prisoners, and a former Borstal boy.

During 1976 alone, the special services included: Profession of Franciscan Brothers; celebration of Jamaica's Independence Day; Mothers' Union Centenary; Royal British Legion; 150th anniversary of the Masonic Province of West Lancashire; Girls' Brigade; Submarine Old Comrades' Association; Dr Barnardo's; Red Cross; Ordination of priests and deacons; Judges' Service; church school leavers; Royal Air Force Association; Liverpool College; BBC Radio Three evensongs; Burma Star Association; Welcome to the

Bishop of Warrington; Admission of Readers; Huyton College; installation of canons; Shelter's tenth anniversary; Boys' Brigade; installation of the Chancellor of the diocese; carols for the handicapped; Trefoil Guild; YMCA and YWCA; Bluecoat School; Picton Scouts; Air Training Corps; carol services for the Townswomen's Guild and four local schools.

Such a list gives a clear indication of the number of occasions when the cathedral is used for services in addition to the 'norm' of liturgical requirements.

Yet perhaps the most special service of the year is that held each May to commemorate the Battle of the Atlantic, the great sea conflict of the Second World War in which the officers and ships defending the Western Approaches were controlled from Liverpool. The cathedral now plans this service in conjunction with the German church on Merseyside. It is seen as an act of reconciliation and love rather than a pageant to the glory of war. 'It demonstrates our Christian duty not only to remember the victims of all sides in the past, but to be peacemakers in the midst of human conflicts and suspicions which are the seeds of war,' says Dean Patey. 'Our ministry to all men is also to recall the sacrifices made in war within the Christian context of faith in the Resurrection.'

The speakers here have included Professor Manek of Czechoslovakia (whose address had to be read because he was refused a visa at the last moment); Philip Noel-Baker, the Nobel Peace Prize winner; Pastor Eberhard Bethge (friend and biographer of Dietrich Bonhoeffer); Pastor Michael Wagner, director of Cimade, the French equivalent of Christian Aid; and Richard Baker, the BBC newscaster.

The Western Rooms, used as an air-raid shelter during the war, were opened for public meetings in the autumn of 1958 when the British Council of Churches held an assembly there. The rooms, which run beneath the Nave, are used free of charge at the Dean's invitation (although this often means that he gives formal approval to requests to hold events there). Over the years they have been a vital centre for the cathedral's 'wider' mission in the community.

13 The majesty of service . . . 'Go to Liverpool Cathedral if you
    want to see how to walk to the glory of God.'

In 1976 groups meeting there were the British Association of Social Workers; Merseyside Marriage Guidance Council; the Muscular Dystrophy Group; Sunday School teachers; Senior Wives; the Church Missionary Society; the Diocesan Synod; North-West Social Work Group; Pathfinders; Social Work Luncheon Club; Evangelical Fellowship; Theological Society; Clergy In-Service Training; Board of Mission and Unity; Royal School of Church Music; and the Diocesan Youth Council.

Liverpool Cathedral exists for all these services and groups; for individuals like the First World War veteran who comes every year to give thanks for his life, saved by the heroic self-sacrifice of Captain Noel Chavasse, twin son of the second Bishop; and for the huge crowds who pack the building for massive thanksgivings. Yet throughout the cathedral's history, the fulfilment of its spiritual role has been under constant scrutiny.

Dean Frederick Dillistone, who followed Dean Dwelly in 1956, said that one of the main tasks was to provide settings for great corporate celebrations. 'When these great occasions come, space and the possibility of free movement are essential and the ceremony gains greatly from the character of its environment. . . . It is so easy for us to take these for granted and yet they only become possible on the great occasion as a result of regular week by week discipline and training through ordinary periods.'

Dillistone was cathedral chancellor for four years before his appointment as second Dean. He was already a widely travelled theologian, having served as a missionary in India and held professorships in theology in Canada and America. He was associated with symbolism and Christian communication, yet was spoken of as being 'very biblical'. He had at first refused the post of dean, but as other candidates left the ratings, either from choice or because they were considered unsuitable, he decided to take the job. Stanley Williams, the cathedral Secretary, recalls: 'I remember Dilly saying one Friday night that we shall know who the new Dean is to be by Monday. On the Monday he told us that he would be pleased to accept the post.'

14 'May I have your autograph, please?' Dr Dillistone, the second Dean, returns to Liverpool and signs for one of his fans.

The new helmsman strengthened the links with local clergy. 'You could tell by the way people talked that there was great affection for him. Somebody was always knocking at his office door,' says Chancellor Naylor. 'It needed a man of great humility to work with people who were themselves so attached to the Dwelly days. You didn't want a man who was going to make noisy pronouncements or antagonize. Dillistone was unobtrusive but firm and he made the cathedral a diocesan home again.' People remember his period of office as 'the calm between two storms'. He was more of a philosopher than his predecessor or the present dean. All three have shown qualities for action and calm, but Dillistone is also remembered as the great mystic.

In 1960 Dr A. H. Crowfoot, a former Dean of Quebec, who had been ordained by Bishop Chavasse in the old pro-cathedral, wrote to 'Dilly': 'You have told us much about the

"Martha" side of the cathedral and all the chair-shifting that these extra services entail. What about the "Mary" side? Of course, it is never the kind of news to make the headlines.'

The Dean answered the question with another question in one of the newsletters which he instigated: 'In a day when vast numbers of people are able to visit our cathedrals and abbeys as tourists, how can it be made clear that a cathedral is primarily a great House of God, rather than just an example of the architect's vision and the craftsman's skills? Our Lord Himself spoke of God's purpose for the Temple, that it should be a house of prayer for all nations, and that purpose, I am sure, holds equally good for this and any other great cathedral.'

Indeed, the cathedral had long since established a 'voice for all nations' via the BBC world service. Not only did it keep exiles of the cathedral company in touch with home, but it showed the excellence of the music and worship to a new audience. A letter from the captain of a British ship in the Far East was typical of the warm response to these early broadcasts: 'You don't know how much it meant to come back on board today, switch on the wireless, and hear that unmistakable Liverpool Cathedral sound. It made me feel that my family, house, and neighbourhood were just around the corner rather than thousands of miles away.'

Television, as we have already seen, was to have an even greater impact. The first televised transmission, by ABC television, was of a Holy Communion service on 13 September 1959. The Press described it as 'the most ambitious religious broadcast ever tackled, including the Coronation'.

Dean Dillistone reported: 'We approach this new departure with a great deal of uncertainty and even apprehension, but no single event in our history, has, as far as I am aware, aroused so much interest and led to so appreciative a response. At least we know that an effective TV programme of the cathedral and its worship is now possible.'

The BBC's first television programme from the cathedral was for Epiphany in 1963, and incorporated musical processions and tableaux. One viewer wrote: 'I thought this was a breakthrough in bringing worship alive in the twentieth century. The beauty of the cathedral was exploited to the full. There was a ballet and poetry about it, but, more importantly, a deep spiritual meaning.' Since those days television cameras have been in the cathedral several times, but the cost of mounting productions with the necessary sound and lighting facilities, prevents frequent use of the television potential.

The televising of that 1959 Communion service was doubly significant. For when Dean Dillistone proposed replacing Matins with the Eucharist as the main Sunday morning service once a month, there was considerable opposition. Many felt that it was nothing short of terrible to give Matins a back seat.

Today, of course, Communion is the main Sunday service at Liverpool and many other cathedrals. In April 1969 Dean Patey said that this great act of worship should no longer be seen as 'a pious and personal optional extra'. And once it became the principal Sunday service, the congregation increased, with many more young people coming along. Yet the intimacy of the Eucharist had caused problems as the cathedral grew in size. The Lady Chapel was ideal for such an act of sharing, and the main cathedral had proved most satisfactory during the early years. But after the Central Space came into use, the celebration was in danger of seeming too remote from the congregation. For some years a temporary altar was fixed up in the East Transept, but the introduction of a new mobile altar in 1965 meant that the Communion idea of 'God in our midst' could be further accentuated. Liverpool now had facilities to demonstrate both the imminent and the transcendent at the Eucharist. The fact that the furniture could be moved around gave a sense of community in its fullest sense, yet the relative distance of the great sandstone reredos of the High Altar, backed by the Te Deum Window, gave the bonus of mystery and 'the Other' which is an acknowledgement at the very heart of all human acts of worship.

The most important development since Dean Dwelly's day has been the working out of what Chancellor Naylor calls the 'eucharistic production'. The clergy and some of the cathedral company (the Cross Guild, etc.) sit facing the congregation, where the Choir meets the East Transept; others sit facing inwards from the sides of the transept. With the congregation facing towards the High Altar, this gives the effect of central-izing the Communion, and of gathering clerical and lay participants around the Table instead of sectionalizing them.

Another important feature is the way in which the candles carried in with the gospel remain on either side of the Gospel Stand during the first part of the service, to highlight the 'Ministry of the Word'. All through this period there are no lights on the Altar Table. At the time of the Offertory, the lights are carried to the Table and set in stands—this time to highlight the 'Ministry of the Sacrament'.

As the Eucharist is now central to so many services—con-firmation, ordination, diocesan and school festivals, etc.—this pattern of worship and ceremonial has to achieve a basic form around which the various service movements can be developed. The value of the Cross Guild in relation to such procedures cannot be overstated: their long-term awareness of the method of worship means that outsiders who are not familiar with the cathedral and the complex movement of its worship, can take part in services without the need for time-consuming rehearsals. This is because Cross Guilders are trained in advance, singly or in groups, and then take charge of clerical and lay processionals in a service, by preceding visitors with a mace to wherever in the building they are required. This system of ceremonial leadership has paid dividends on countless occasions: notable examples in recent years have been the completion service attended by the Queen and Prince Philip, and the installation of Bishop David Sheppard in June 1975.

The conception of the Cross Guild was at the very centre of Dwelly's administrative success. He did not want to capture the imagination of young choirboys and then discard their active participation when their voices had broken. Instead, he would harness their enthusiasm and expand it.

Another person who felt the same was Wirral-born Francis Neilson, who first fell in love with Liverpool Cathedral after

15 The enthronement of Stuart Blanch, now Archbishop of York, as Bishop of Liverpool.

the First World War. When he returned to this country in the 1930s, after a number of years in America, he fully approved of what Dwelly was doing—'a symphony in music, colour, and movement'. He set up a Trust to provide for the musical education of choirboys (the cathedral still pays for a boy to learn to play an instrument of his choice). Money from the Trust has also been used for special activities, and to provide facilities for the Cross Guild. Neilson addressed himself to the choirboys in a most touching letter: 'For you to realize how much you are part of the glorious scheme of things is like a duty endowed as a gift. It really means that, if you are fully conscious of the worth of your service, an avenue is opened which you will never forsake. . . . There should be no broken period in the sequence of your purpose. When your voice changes, the vocation is not at an end, for the Cross Guild stands ready to receive you.'

At the time, there was nothing similar within the English Cathedral tradition, although the idea has now been borrowed elsewhere. Today, there are hundreds of former choristers who qualify for membership, and a hard core of fifty or sixty can be readily called on by the founder president, Mr Bunny Hunter, to take part in services. Two names on the list of Guild members are those of the present organist, Noel Rawsthorne and the choirmaster, Ronald Woan. They are the only men alive who can claim to have been involved with the music of a Gothic cathedral for more than half of its history. And they are working in one of the few cathedrals in the world where the posts of organist and choirmaster are split in this way. That was another Liverpool innovation. The Chapter wanted an excellent organist and a strong choir, and their foresight has achieved both. In this way Noel Rawsthorne has found ample time to become an internationally acclaimed recitalist and is one of only two British organists to have toured the USSR. When he succeeded Harry Goss Custard in 1955 and took charge of the noblest church organ in the world, he was only twenty-five. 'The nine-year apprenticeship I served under Goss in the organ loft was invaluable,' he recalls. 'Meanwhile, the cathedral was paying for my

16 Beatle Paul McCartney (fourth from left) at a choir audition in 1953. He was rejected!

organ lessons.' Later he was to study in Rome with Fernando Germani and in Paris with Marcel Dupré. Now his recordings of the cathedral organ music sell by the thousand and his recitals attract capacity audiences.

Ronald Woan, although at one time a practising organist, has long since given up playing, and is able to devote all his time to choir training. He has been doing this work since 1948, when he took over from Edgar Robinson, a former chorister at Lincoln Cathedral. He recruits boys from local schools, auditioning up to twenty candidates per term. He well remembers an audition back in 1953, when a boy called Paul McCartney was unsuccessful in his attempts to join. Young McCartney, of course, went on to create a different Mersey Sound with pals John Lennon, George Harrison, and Ringo Starr!

'We are not in the position of King's College, Cambridge or St George's Chapel, Windsor where boys audition from choir schools and can sing an aria from the *Messiah* at the age of nine,' says Woan. 'We take them raw and train them up from scratch.'

Today's choir is made up of twenty-four singing boys (excluding probationers and juniors) and fifteen men, plus some undergraduates from Liverpool University on student-ships. Unlike many cathedrals, which have daily sung services, Liverpool uses its choir only on Fridays, Saturdays, and Sundays.

There have been some interesting musical milestones. Special music written for the cathedral during the early years included works by Martin Shaw and Christopher Le Flemyng. Later, names such as Kenneth Leighton and Peter Dickinson were to make their mark, while at the same time the amount of 'home-grown' music increased. The choir now have in their repertoire service settings by Noel Rawsthorne, assistant organist Ernest Pratt, deputy choirmaster David Moore, Cross Guilder John Madden, and so on.

But there has always been an equal regard for the historical tradition of music in worship. An edition of the complete works of William Byrd, paid for by and dedicated to the cathedral, has played a vital part in the whole renaissance of interest in Tudor music. During the 1930s the cathedral choir was considered *avant-garde* in its performances of the works of composers like Vaughan Williams and Holst. In the 1970s they are everyday service and anthem settings. At Liverpool you can hear everything from Palestrina to Series III Com-munion, although the big verse anthems by Travers, Crotch, Wesley, and others are gradually going by the board with the increasing emphasis on brevity and impact in worship.

In a wider context, the choir has combined with others at the cathedral and elsewhere in massive choral works per-formed with the Royal Liverpool Philharmonic Orchestra, many of them conducted by Sir Charles Groves. (During his fourteen years on Merseyside, before becoming musical director of English National Opera, Sir Charles was a regular worshipper at the cathedral, and loved to do concerts there.)

Victims of inflation latterly have been Ronald Woan's Cathedral Singers, founded in 1958. They became famous for renderings of the Bach Passions. 'To hear that music in a darkening cathedral on Good Friday evening, with a single light focused on the High Altar reredos, was one of the great emotional experiences of my life,' says Woan.

The fountain of all this musical activity was Dwelly, who at one stage formed a College of Counsel, in which he unashamedly picked the brains of some of the leading arts figures of the day, including Martin Shaw and John Masefield. Worship, music, movement were the tools which Dwelly used, and they are still being used with full effect today. He believed that 'people worship in tiny pieces through the hour', and that to create the conditions of those moments of other-worldliness was his prime task.

Liverpool Cathedral can probably claim to be the most exciting religious laboratory in the world. Quite apart from the sure knowledge that its presentation of worship is vigorous and thought-provoking, there is the indisputable asset of the sheer grandeur offered by the fabric. One can only echo Dean Dwelly's famous exhortation, when he would encourage children to lie on the floor or on chairs: 'Look up! Look up!' This cathedral is a sanctuary, a workshop, and a theatre of faith. We are fortunate to have had a succession of deans who were fully aware of each aspect.

7

Odium Theologicum

In placing the interests of religion first, and the
interests of church policy second, you have lit a
candle in the Church of England that will not easily
be put out. . . . You have great allies and they will not
desert you.

DR L. P. JACKS

Most cathedrals have had their share of real-life drama—
from the murder of Becket at Canterbury to the bombing of
Coventry during the Second World War. But the person-to-
person drama which centred on Liverpool Cathedral during
1933 and 1934 can have few, if any, rivals for the intensity of
conflict it unearthed or the courage it revealed. It is a story
which is brutal and compassionate, bigoted and far-sighted
by turns; an episode where the letter of the law won a technical victory over the charity of men's hearts, but where the real
victory is only now being fully realized. On the one hand it is
a story of deep-rooted, almost medieval darkness which, had
it known a parallel in the Middle Ages, would probably have
resulted in the Bishop and the Dean of Liverpool being
sentenced to the block. On the other hand, it is also a tale of
hope and pastoral leadership, emerging from 'piracy' on the
'high see'.

The principal characters in the drama were two Unitarian
preachers; two archbishops; the Bishop, Dean and Chapter of
Liverpool Cathedral; and a Member of Parliament. Extras'
parts were taken by miscellaneous bishops and deans, as well
as preachers throughout the land. And, of course, there was
the Great British Public. So much for the prologue; let us
proceed to the plot.

As an act of Christian good will, Dean Dwelly had invited
the famous Unitarian preacher, Dr L. P. Jacks, Editor of the
Hibbert Journal, to give addresses at three cathedral services

on 4, 11 and 18 June 1933. These were special 'non-liturgical' People's Services at 8.30 pm. Four months later, on 22 October, Dwelly also invited the Unitarian minister Lawrence Redfern, from a neighbouring Liverpool church, to speak at an 'ordinary' morning service, attended by judges of the Assize Court. Both accepted and carried out their commitments. But within three days of Redfern's address, fire and brimstone were being rained on the cathedral, and a controversy was thus begun which became the *cause célèbre* of twentieth-century Anglican politics and filled hundreds of columns in the local and national Press. There can be no doubt that many side issues and prejudices were brought into the open. Yet there was also a tremendous response from people who wished to discuss the definition of their respective faiths.

One of the opening volleys was fired by Roger Markham, rector of Aughton, near Ormskirk. He wrote to the *Liverpool Daily Post*: 'Unitarianism is a heresy which strikes at the very foundation of the Christian faith by denying in any real sense the incarnation of the Son of God. . . . The whole conception of God and His relationship to humanity is at stake.'

And talking of stakes, the North Meols Ruridecanal Conference in Southport put out a statement saying that 'some of us would rather go to the stake than admit them [Unitarians] to our pulpits'.

Critics expressed the view that many people would not have given to the cathedral building fund had they foreseen the situation. One Merseyside vicar asked that if 'lawlessness' was praiseworthy in the Dean and Chapter, what would be the reaction if other parishes in the diocese followed the example of the mother church?

Canon Lancelot (not a bad name when you are engaged in fighting talk), the Rural Dean of North Meols, said that many non-Church of England donors had contributed to the cathedral, but the building had not been erected 'as a sort of civic temple, where all sorts and conditions of people might get a hearing'. He added that the move was 'utterly subversive of faith and order as we Church of England people have known it all our lives'.

And the North Meols statement said with a complicated mixture of threat and panic: 'There are those in our midst who temperamentally are ready subjects for the Church of Rome with its claim of steady witness and authoritative truth, but who remain with us in somewhat uneasy allegiance. What must they think?... Is the true beacon of light in the Liverpool diocese to shine out not from St James's Mount, but from Mount Pleasant [the site of the Metropolitan Cathedral crypt]?

North Meols was not alone in its motion of regret. The rural deaconries of Bootle and Ormskirk also passed protest resolutions. But cries of 'Shame' from clerics and ordinary laymen lacked the weight of what could be classed as objective and official disapproval. Yet such a champion was to hand in the person of Hugh Richard Heathcote Gascoyne Cecil, Baron Quickswood, fifth and youngest son of the third Marquis of Salisbury.

Lord Hugh Cecil, who had served as MP for Greenwich from 1895 until 1906, when his backing for Free Trade unseated him, led a life devoted to Anglican principles and Conservative politics. His brother William became Bishop of Exeter, but as the son of a former prime minister, Hugh preferred the arena of public debate. He helped to create the Church Assembly, but his advocacy was that of the ecclesiastical lawyer rather than the angel. Associates spoke of his forensic logic, often so rigid as to exclude a sense of charity. Cecil may have been on the side of personal liberty, but his vision was of a liberty strait-jacketed by unbending rules. (At the age of seven he is said to have indicated his nurse as a Socinian, and admitted that he himself had not been quite orthodox!) One of the great failures of his life was in trying to persuade the Church not to marry divorcees.

It was Cecil, all ice-cold logic and iron-hard will, who brought the cathedral controversy to a head. He told a London meeting of the Church Assembly's House of Laity that he deplored the 'present anarchy' in the Church of England and had attended services which were most irregular. Unitarians in the pulpit of Liverpool Cathedral constituted 'a grave scandal'.

On the same day, 13 November, a public meeting organized by the English Church Union at Church House, Liverpool said that the cathedral's action did not 'assist the cause for reunion'.

As Christmas approached, the season of good will to all men appeared to be receding: on 22 December the news broke that Cecil had decided to begin proceedings under church law against the Bishop and the Dean. The issue under debate was the status of Unitarians within the Christian community. It was a debate based on the Nicene Creed of AD 325, as Unitarians would not state that Christ 'was one substance with the Father'. Was Christ the One Incarnate, or was there a succession of incarnations through the ages? The same sort of issues had been raised between the Arians and the Catholics in the fourth century. In Liverpool, history was repeating itself with equal fervour.

Cecil decided to petition the Archbishop of York, Dr Temple, to set up a tribunal to hear the issue. He also wrote to Bishop David, making charges against Dwelly. Cecil alleged that the invitation procedure had been contrary to the Church Discipline Act of 1840. In his letter to the Archbishop he noted that while the Bishop had approved the approach to Dr Jacks on the biblical basis of 'He that is not against us is with us', he had not consented to or approved the invitation to Redfern.

While correspondence raged in the Press, Redfern gave a measured reply, saying that the whole outlook of the cathedral was affected. 'I accepted the invitation with a sense of profound thankfulness, as a gesture of Christian brotherliness . . . and as further evidence of the truth that the doctrines which divide may yet be held with the faith that unites.'

Dr C. E. Raven, Regius Professor of Divinity at Cambridge and Chancellor Emeritus of the cathedral, said that the spiritual message of God could not be delivered only with the ancient forms and methods.

At the time of the consecration of the building, Raven had set down the following words: 'The conception of the cathedral, as embodying the Godward aspiration of our civic life, should control its future uses. Its character is not that of a glorified parish church.

'It is in a unique sense the spiritual home of the people of Liverpool, and should serve particularly to express their corporate devotion to God and their fellowship one with another.

'The cathedral should be above sectional and divisive influences and be able to unite us all in whatever makes for true service to God and man.... It should be a centre for unity, where all can sink their divisions in the sole adoration of Him in whom there is neither Jew nor Greek.'

And in an early history of the cathedral, Raven wrote: 'Religion is not static, but dynamic and adventurous, not as a system of duties, but a way of living.'

It was clear from the beginning that the cathedral was to be governed by love and not by law, and that to appeal from the spirit of the constitution to its letter, would, in effect, be a breach of fellowship and a betrayal of trust. All that was happening was merely a carrying out of those hopes. But others did not see it that way.

In a cathedral sermon on 31 December, Raven said the issue had 'a significance for the whole future of man's spiritual advance'. Free Christians was the title many Unitarians would choose for themselves. Jacks, Redfern, and their colleagues were in the fullest sense ministers of Christ. Meanwhile, the Unitarians were coming through the battle well. They showed humility and restraint. Redfern, however, stirred up a hornets' nest when he asked, in a sermon at his own church, how many men could say that they accepted all thirty-nine articles of faith. Not many, he suspected.

At this stage, letters to the Press were balanced in Cecil's favour, although in the New Year of 1934, a leading church newspaper appealed for the matter to be dropped. 'Strife among fellow churchmen is always deplorable and seldom, if ever, leads to any good,' said the editorial. In some ways the heat seemed to be dying down. Bishop David announced that he would not take proceedings against Dwelly as Cecil had requested. 'No preacher invited here has ever transgressed the honourable understanding not to question Anglican doctrine, nor would we, in any case, invite one whom we could not trust to restrict himself to common ground.'

Two days later, on 7 January, the Bishop told a cathedral congregation: 'We have learned to judge a man by what he affirms rather than by what he denies.' If the Church was to live, lead, and save, it must grow free in the interpretation of doctrine, yet remain faithful to ancient teaching. A rigid stand on the form of words would make doctrine a ring fence instead of a signpost.

Cecil was furious with the Bishop's reply. As the issue was a spiritual one, he would not seek the authority of the state or the courts to settle it, but would press to bring it to the attention of whatever church authority he could.

Just as some ministers of the Free Churches were beginning to back Dwelly's initiative, the *Liverpool Post* announced on 18 January that in a fortnight's time the Archbishop of York was to speak on the controversy in his presidential address to the Joint Synod of the Convocation of York, and that it would also be discussed by the Lower House of Convocation. The Archbishop was concerned that it might seem that the Church of England was delaying on its stance. The publicity had involved the risk, he said, of making ill-informed people doubt the firmness of the Church's adherence to the Catholic faith of Christendom in Jesus as 'Very God'. The whole episode illustrated the danger of division and disruption, by the present inability to revise canon law so that it might be applied directly to the issues of the day. It was urgently necessary, admitted Dr Temple, to let the Church obtain freedom to fashion the laws of worship to immediate needs.

Exactly what fellowship could be entertained with people who did not share the Catholic faith, awaited further determination. And he added that true fellowship was only possible 'with those who are united with us at that point'. In a salient passage Dr Temple said that he did not regard the phrase 'Christian Communion' as including Unitarians when he introduced his resolution of 1922 on members of other Christian bodies joining in services in consecrated buildings.

Ironically, the Bishop of Liverpool was not at convocation; he was on holiday for health reasons, and further discussion could only take place when he was present.

Elsewhere the debate carried on. The most vitriolic condemnation of Lord Hugh Cecil's action came in the *St Martin Review*, the magazine of St Martin-in-the-Fields, parish church of the Royal Household.

The Revd Pat McCormick said it was all the more ominous because Cecil was regarded as a very representative churchman. 'We dissent passionately from the latest issue he has thought it right to advance.

'If, in this business, Lord Hugh Cecil must go on the warpath with bow and arrow, our heretical scalp should be included in his medieval museum. For we too have gladly asked Dr Jacks to preach in our church. We should be happy to be catalogued in the museum exhibits as Jonathan alongside Dr David.

'Lord Hugh Cecil should go the whole hog and arraign every heretic. What are Doctors David and Dwelly among so many?

'Why may not a cathedral or a parish church give a warm, if occasional, hearing to a man as noble and righteous as Dr Jacks . . . one of the major prophets of our time?

'The attitude of those who declare that goodness and wisdom must recast themselves in their own particular mould before their speaking can be attended to within the House of God, seems to us in blood relationship to be the ugly sin of persecution. Any custom or canon law must go by the board if it is not in line with the spirit of Christ.'

The gulf of opinion in the Church of England was widening and becoming ever more embarrassing. There was extensive feeling that Dr Temple had missed a valuable opportunity to bring Church and people closer together.

Redfern told the spring General Assembly of the Unitarian and Free Churches in London that we were in the midst of 'perhaps a momentous phase' in the great religious turmoil of history. 'Circumstances change, the conflict goes on. It is the condition of all religious progress,' he concluded. At the same conference the president, the Revd Alfred Hall of Sheffield, said: 'We value more than words can tell the liberal-mindedness, the honesty of the Bishop of Liverpool and Dean Dwelly, and of the modern churchmen who have ably and nobly supported our attitude.'

The drama was approaching its climax. Dr David was now able to attend convocation and when the bishops of the Northern Province met in York in June, the Liverpool debate dominated the proceedings. Temple reminded everyone that what was happening bore 'no resemblance to a trial'. For his part, Dr David said that some of the reaction had been hysterical, but he conceded that the decision would be made by the 'voice of the living Church'.

On 7 June, the Upper House of Convocation, with twelve bishops voting unanimously, passed a resolution forbidding invitations to Unitarian preachers to occupy Church of England pulpits at special or non-liturgical services. Bishop David, who was himself opposed to Unitarians addressing ordinary services, warned in his reply that some would regard the vote as a real disaster. He said that the invitation had been to an individual and not to a representative of a religious body.

The media generally backed the decision with their editorial comment, and the following month, the Archbishop of Canterbury, Cosmo Lang, speaking to the Canterbury diocesan conference on the 'Visible Unity of the Church of Christ', said that Anglicans had a distinctive heritage of faith 'which could not be bartered away', even for the sake of unity.

There had been recently disclosed tendencies which seemed to whittle away existing differences in an endeavour to reach some lowest common denominator of agreement, and so far as the Church of England was concerned, to empty it of distinctive character and witness. If happenings at Liverpool Cathedral had passed without some authoritative protest, it might have seemed that a vital truth of Christ's Deity was so lightly esteemed that even its explicit denial was not regarded as a disqualification for admission to Anglican pulpits.

The Bishop of Durham, Hensley Henson, who had laid the resolution before convocation, felt obliged to add comments in a booklet published that summer: Unitarianism and historic Christianity could not be harmonized. Those who did not expressly share the creed of the Anglican Church and administer its sacraments, could not be admitted to its pulpits.

The Bishop of Gloucester, Dr A. C. Headlam, also weighed in: the action of the Bishop and the Dean of Liverpool seemed to him to 'represent, from the point of view of policy, an error, and from the point of view of Christian faith, an offence to believing Christians'. It was, he said in his diocesan newsletter, 'inconsistent with the purpose of the building'.

Back in Liverpool, Dr David also took to print in his *Liverpool Review*: 'The Upper House has decided that invitations to give addresses at special services must be restricted by the conditions that govern invitations to Non-Conformists to preach at regular services of the Church. As I have already said, I shall conform to this decision.

'In making it, however, the House found itself (reluctantly, I think) compelled to declare by implication that Unitarians are not for this purpose to be reckoned as "members of the Christian communion". In this exclusion I do not, and shall never, acquiesce. On the debate itself, I would make a first and final comment: it was largely a defence of a Christian doctrine which nobody had attacked.'

Despite his apparent resilience, Bishop David was left with wounds to lick. When the Bishop of Durham's draft resolutions were published, it was clear that the Jacks case was to be considered not so much as a breach of Christian order, but rather as an act tending to subvert Christian belief. One clause, although later withdrawn, suggested by inference that Bishop David had been guilty of disloyalty to the Catholic faith. The wording had been widely circulated, and Dr David felt that it had done him harm which could never be entirely repaired.

Dean Dwelly, who had taken something of a backseat position in the weeks leading up to the York decision, was now in the thick of it all once more.

On 18 June Canon T. Davey, a residentiary canon of Liverpool Cathedral, climbed the steps to the pulpit and amazed his listeners by reading an apology to Dr Jacks from Dwelly and Raven.

Only three days earlier Lord Hugh Cecil had written to Archbishop Temple withdrawing the petition asking him to take action against Bishop David. The York decision had satisfied him.

But then the Dean and Chancellor Emeritus of Liverpool determined to play the trump card:

'Dear Dr Jacks—We beg to express publicly our deep sense of regret and of remorse for the humiliation to which our invitation and your gracious acceptance of it, have exposed you. That as a result of your fine spirit of Christian neighbourliness, your status as a Christian should have been impugned. That out of an act of fellowship, there should have arisen this outburst of odium theologicum, is to us a matter of which we are bitterly ashamed ... Those who note the contrast between the Archbishop's [Temple's] utterances on the occasion and his speeches in former years, will have his faith in episcopacy rudely shaken.'

Dwelly and Raven noted that the spirit and method of heresy hunters in the Church had proved disastrous in the long term. The present attempt to exclude those who did not conform to the findings of the 1927 Lausanne Conference was not far from blasphemy against the Holy Spirit. (Lausanne was a worldwide conference of Christians which formulated a common confession of faith, and in which the second finding was: In the centre of the gospel stands Jesus Christ, Son of God and Son of Man, who through his death and resurrection has redeemed mankind and brought life and immortality to light.)

Dr Jacks's reply, read at the same service, was equally spectacular. Because of its undoubted importance (the Dean had it specially printed) in relation to an 'outside' view of mission at Liverpool Cathedral, no apology is made for quoting it at length: 'The general effect of your letter on my mind is to confirm a long-held conviction that unless the churches of Christendom are able to transcend their institutional selfishness, their corporate self-seeking and uncharitable relations among themselves, learning to help rather than hinder one another, and to bear each other's burdens instead of increasing them; unless, that is, they are willing to put religion before church politics, the days of organized Christianity are most assuredly numbered. How seldom has any of them played the part of the Good Samaritan to any other . . .

"On the one side of the line," said the Bishop of Durham, in introducing the resolution subsequently adopted by the Convocation of York, "stands the Holy Catholic Church. On the other stand the Unitarians". What sentence of excommunication could be more explicit? . . . Unitarians must now regard themselves as definitely excluded from Anglican pulpits. The intention was, simply, to lock the Anglican gate against the risk of Unitarian trespass.

'As to the check you have received in Liverpool Cathedral from the resolution, I count it no more than what the pioneers of spiritual progress must constantly expect in the course of their service.

'At most the check will be temporary, and may even be found, when the final account is taken, not to have been a check at all, but a step in bringing you nearer to your goal. I feel convinced it will be so.

'. . . I think that the Convocation of York, with Archbishop Temple at its head, are entitled to sympathy for having had this question forced upon them at the present time. Publicly confronted with the question: May known Unitarians preach in your cathedrals? there is only one answer that could be expected. It was bound to be "No".

'Unitarians, at least, know what to expect when summoned before a theological court martial. And yet the bishops must have known that, however correctly their negative answer interpreted the theological basis of their Church, it was certain to provoke unfavourable reactions from an immense multitude of thoughtful people, who, though not professedly Unitarians, are by no means whole-hearted in their acceptance of the Nicene Creed, but feel, nevertheless, that the cathedral of a great city is fulfilling its rightful function when it offers them a religious home and spiritual food they can accept.

'. . . To me, as one of the multitude just mentioned, the decision of Convocation seems correct as an official utterance, but remote from reality. *Per contra*, the aims of Liverpool Cathedral seem close to reality, but doubtfully correct in the official sense. I think the balance is in your favour. The Church of England has done itself an injury in expressing disapproval of your action.

'In placing the interests of religion first, and the interests of church policy second, you have lit a candle in the Church of England that will not easily be put out. The light of it will have a far penetration both in time and in space. It will be seen and welcomed by an immense multitude of Christians, not professedly Unitarians, but no more bound to the Creed of Nicaea than they, whom the Bishop of Durham's resolution, if taken seriously, would render outcast from the Visible Church. And beyond these are the masses of our fellow subjects in the East—the Hindu, the Buddhist, the Moslem, to be counted in the total hundreds of millions, for whom the appeal of organized Christianity is so often sterilized by the spectacle of its internal divisions and by its attitude of exclusiveness, if not reprobation, to all that lies outside itself.

'The spiritual men of India, a great and watchful multitude, whose spiritual status is unassailable, many of them Catholics in a deeper sense than we of the West have yet given to the word, these, Mr Dean, will note what you have done and they will hold Liverpool Cathedral in high honour.

'. . . How then, Mr Dean, can I have a grievance against you for associating me with Liverpool Cathedral in a course of action so entirely in harmony with the deeper needs of our time? I am deeply sensible of the difficult position in which you are placed by the Bishop of Durham's resolution.

'If henceforward you are to be restricted in your choice of preachers from outside, to Non-Conformists whose membership of the Visible Church is guaranteed by unequivocal acceptance of the Creed of Nicaea, I am afraid you will find the area of selection not very large to begin with and continually diminishing as time goes on; you may even encounter doubtful cases among eminent members of the Church of England.

'But I cannot believe that the high aims of Liverpool Cathedral will be defeated by a restriction so impossible to observe. You have great allies and they will not desert you.

'There can be no question that Convocation is on firm ground when it asserts that the ancient cathedrals of England are historically bound up with the theology of Nicaea. No one who enters these shrines and notes their manner of adoring the Deity can fail to see that they are temples of Christ worship as defined by the Nicaean formula.

'But some qualification of these statements seems to be needed in the case of Liverpool Cathedral, a creation of the modern world, and one of its noblest. I doubt, Mr Dean, if the citizens of your great city would be generally content to regard the cathedral you serve as a fortress of the Nicene Creed, and of the view of the universe implied in it, which involves, among other things, the Ptolemaic astronomy.

'A sense of this, I confess, was strong in my mind when I accepted your fraternal invitation to speak at the special services. Had Archbishop Temple invited me to speak in York Minster, or Bishop Henson in Durham Cathedral, or sanctioned an invitation from the Dean, I think I should have prayed to be excused, as feeling myself too out of place in either.

'But somehow it was different when the invitation came from you in Liverpool. I reflected that Liverpool has a somewhat different manner of life, and a different outlook on the universe, from that of our ancient cathedral cities, and something of the Liverpool spirit, which I lived long enough in the city to imbibe, took possession of me. I was therefore unvisited by the misgivings which I should have had in the other cases, that I might not feel at home.

'The Convocation of York has now decided that I was a trespasser; but at the time, with your invitation and the Bishop's sanction behind it, I seemed, to myself, to have a sufficient passport.'

Redfern, who was to receive a similar letter of apology on 24 June, had just spoken at the Unitarian Synod in Belfast, and said that the tremendous discovery which the world of religion was making, and of which the cathedral controversy was one expression, was that a religion which aspires to be free was under the only true authority—that of the spirit. 'Creeds come and go and controversies disturb for a time the hearts of the living and the dust of the dead, but somehow in our Christian temples we become one Christian brotherhood. No man can be excluded from the true Church, save by the death of goodness in his own heart.'

Replying to Dwelly and Raven's apology, Redfern said: 'Unwittingly, you have broken the law. Unwittingly, I was an accessory. I seem to remember that Peter and the Apostles did the same when they preached the Way in the precincts of the temple. Authority was outraged and the world was shocked, but the world's blame has long ago turned to reverence.'

The letters of apology caused their own mini-scandal at the cathedral and a new row broke out among the clergy. Members of the Principal Chapter wrote to the local newspapers saying that the apology controverted the York decision and was deeply regretted. 'We do not recognize the right of any individual member of the Chapter, and certainly not the right of Professor Raven, who is not a member, to speak in the name of the cathedral,' they said.

When Raven asserted that arrangements for special services were under the charge of the Dean alone (who had consulted him), his successor, Chancellor J. S. Bezzant, replied that under statute any disagreement among the Chapter on special or ordinary services would be referred to the Bishop, whose decision was final. Bezzant added the sting that he could not find any specific duties laid down for the Chancellor Emeritus.

Bishop David was continually called upon by the media to act as referee. He wrote to the *Liverpool Post* saying that it had been right to apologize to Jacks and Redfern. But three mistakes had been made: the apologies controverted the York decision; they gave the impression that the Chapter wished to carry on the argument against it; and one of the apologies was read at a cathedral service.

Perhaps not surprisingly, Dwelly, the man who administered the Cathedral, was to have the last word. In a cathedral address on 1 July 1934, he told the congregation: 'Loyal obedience dictates that until further orders are issued by authority, I must find other ways of expressing and deepening the greater fellowship.' He went on: 'Since the welfare of this cathedral church requires that those who bear rule in this holy place should not again be embarrassed, I shall not, until further order, presume to rely upon any claim which has no binding authority in law.'

The actual controversy may have ended, but its effects smouldered on for years. Yet relationships with members of the Free Churches have always prospered at the cathedral. The congregation from the Church of Scotland, now unable to use their unsafe building in nearby Rodney Street, hold their services in the cathedral's Western Rooms.

Back in the summer of 1937, 2,000 people representing Anglican and Non-Conformist churches packed into the building for what the Press described as 'a unique, even historic service'. A further 4,300 applicants had to be turned down because of lack of space (the completed area of the cathedral was much smaller then).

Dwelly seized on the opportunity afforded by the service being broadcast to the Empire, for a little worthwhile retrospection. The service, he said, was 'designed to avoid the disquiet which people felt if ministers of other churches were invited to take part in a regular service of the Church of England, or to preach in an Anglican pulpit'. He continued: 'On the other hand there is a vast body of Christians to whom it is intolerable that those who worship the One Divine Father should never be allowed to do so publicly and together.' The service was 'one of worship, prayer, and praise, and of affirmation of the deep unity which exists with representatives of Christians who have striven to increase it'.

Over the years, members of the Free Churches have responded freely to the fellowship offered by the Chapter of

Liverpool Cathedral. They have come along to sing, pray, and take the Eucharist with their Christian brothers.

In more recent times Kenneth Slack, Moderator of the United Reformed Church, had this to say in a service at Norwich Cathedral: 'Archbishop Geoffrey Fisher tried to break the post-war ecumenical deadlock by asking the Free Churches to take episcopacy into their systems. Could you carry on the good work of getting us to take cathedrals into our systems? The vision rises before my eyes of a cathedral whose Chapter has been joined by representative men from the Free Churches, and, if their discipline should allow, by Roman Catholics.'

Dean Patey considered Slack's statement fundamental to the future needs of the Church and printed it in his newsletter. Liverpool has been making such noises for years, although everyone knew that to make real inroads towards unity, good will and fellowship had to be established with the Church of Rome—especially in Liverpool, with its hard core of Irish Catholics.

8

Ecumenical Cathedral

> Half a century ago, two cathedrals in such close proximity would have been interpreted in terms of ecclesiastical rivalry. Today, at both ends of Hope Street, we rejoice at the new ecumenical spirit which has rightly been described as the great new fact of our era.
>
> EDWARD PATEY

The consecration of Liverpool's Roman Catholic Cathedral on Whit Sunday 1967, was an event of significance for the whole Christian community on Merseyside. Apart from anything else, the cathedrals were too close together to ignore each other: Liverpool Cathedral (it is incorrect to refer to it as the 'Anglican' Cathedral) and the Metropolitan Cathedral of Christ the King, were less than a mile apart, facing each other down Hope Street.

It was the late Cardinal Heenan, then Archbishop of Liverpool, who inverted the title and incorporated it into the frequently quoted phrase of 'a street called Hope'. This statement has provided the banner beneath which the cathedrals have sought a deeper relationship. But more than a decade later, it has not gone very far beyond the level of lip service. This is because the pyramidal authority of both churches has yet to open the gateway to true ecumenism. There is also the basic fear, by no means peculiar to Liverpool, that unity requires one or both of the bodies to lose something of their special status and identity.

However, it would be unwise, and unfair, to ignore the progress which has been made in the sphere of public relations. During the summer of 1963, Archbishop Heenan had visited Dean Dillistone for tea and made the observation: 'The two cathedrals may be taken to symbolize the spirit of Liverpool. Unlike in design, they soar above the city, not as rivals, but as twin monuments to the religious fervour of a great Christian city.' He was talking of an urban mass of more than two million people, the numbers of Anglicans and Roman Catholics divided on a virtual fifty-fifty basis. This equality of numbers was a great boon to the dialogue which was developing between church leaders.

Yet Liverpool was also the city of the Orange and Green processions which were spawned by history and thereafter became demonstrations of strength as well as an excuse for a jolly good day out! Demonstrations of a darker kind too have occurred in the era of the two cathedrals. When it was learned that the Auxiliary Bishop of Liverpool, Augustine Harris, had been asked to preach at a service in January 1968, the British Council of Protestant Christian Churches asked to meet Patey. Their letter said: 'By having the priest of Rome in one of our Protestant churches, it accredits him as being a Christian minister . . .'

In a strongly worded reply, the Dean remarked: 'The tremendous and thrilling experience of unity inside the cathedral that evening, appeared to many to be a greater manifestation of the Spirit of God at work than the rather sad and pathetic demonstration organized by your council outside in the dark. Had you come into the cathedral, I would have suggested that we went into a quiet corner, not to argue, but to pray.'

On one occasion, the words of John Ryle, the first Bishop of Liverpool—'Beware of countenancing any retrograde movement in the country towards Rome'—were thrown back in Patey's face by the Liverpool branch of the British Constitutional Defence Council, whose chairman was none other than the Revd Ian Paisley. (These are the people who sent the Dean a copy of their leaflet called *The Ecumenical Ship Sails Again—Christians Beware.*) Over the years they were to complain to Patey quite frequently, expressing disappointment with his actions. When they suggested that the Dean should arrange a public meeting to discuss unity, Patey consulted Bishop Blanch, who replied privately that as far as he was concerned, such a suggestion was 'simply not on'.

The Defence Council deplored the move to have Arch-bishop George Beck address a hospitals service, and called for the invitation to be withdrawn. Patey, they claimed, was helping to destroy the Anglican Church. As it happened, Beck was in hospital and unable to preach. Patey pointed out that the hospitals service was non-denominational and broad-cast to patients of all beliefs. The year before (1969), the Bishop of Chester had spoken at the same service in the Metropolitan Cathedral. 'The ecumenical policies to which your members object, are not my own individual whims. Not only are they supported by the Bishop of Liverpool and the Cathedral Chapter, but also officially by the Church of England through its duly constituted councils and assem-blies,' said Patey. 'The Ecumenical Movement is, in fact, one to which the Church of England is wholly committed by its official representatives on the World Council of Churches.'

Prior to Bishop Sheppard's enthronement in the summer of 1975, the Defence Council sought assurances that the service would not include invitations to Roman Catholic clergy. 'We have a right to insist that the ceremony will be a truly Christian one in every way,' they said.

In another incident, a petition bearing 6,000 names was left on the Communion Table when Father Kevin Kelly, Profes-sor of Moral Theology at Up Holland College, Wigan was shouted down. The Lord Mayor of the day, himself an Anglican, snubbed the petitioners as they tried to give him the list of signatures.

When the cathedrals held a joint act of worship on 5 June 1977, to mark the occasion of the Queen's Silver Jubilee, a small group of protesters yelled 'No Roman rule' and 'Our Queen is Protestant' as the multi-denominational congrega-tion left St James's Mount to walk in procession with the Salvation Army Band to the Metropolitan Cathedral. Bishop Sheppard said the outburst was 'utterly irrelevant' and Archbishop Derek Worlock commented: 'We are growing together all the time and our bond gets stronger daily. We all have an ability to sink differences.'

But the major ecumenical revolt had been when Cardinal

Jan Willebrands, President of the Vatican Secretariat for Christian Unity, spoke at a special evening service in the cathedral. Willebrands, now Roman Catholic primate of Holland, came to Liverpool at the suggestion of the Revd Rex Kissack, President of the Merseyside Free Church Federal Council, who had attended the Vatican Council as a Methodist observer. The night before at Lambeth Palace he had been the guest of the Archbishop of Canterbury, Michael Ramsay, who had warned him of possible trouble. The Archbishop was not to be proved wrong. Between 400 and 500 protesters inside the cathedral cried out 'No popery! Go back to Rome!' as Patey introduced him to the congregation. Then, when Willebrands went to the pulpit, the reaction was even rowdier. It was decided to fire the cathedral's ultimate deterrent—the full power of the organ—at the demonstrators. The music completely obliterated the shouts, and twenty minutes later, when the troublemakers had been escorted from the building by stewards, Willebrands gave his sermon.

The only other incident that evening had been earlier: as Archbishop Beck was reading a text from the Jerusalem Bible, a group of people stood up and read the same passage, simultaneously, from the King James Bible.

If the Orange and evangelical factions turned up to disrupt Roman Catholic participation in services, they were to experience another thorny problem when dealing directly with Patey for their own purposes. In December 1975 the Grand Lodge Juvenile Committee of the Loyal Orange Institution of England asked if they could hold a service the following June for 2,000 children from all over Britain. It was planned as part of the Orange Lodge Centenary Celebrations, and the letter added: 'We would consider it an honour if our Bishop David Sheppard would preach the sermon.' But Patey refused. The Order was widely known to be opposed to the Roman Catholic Church. The Cathedral Chapter did not share the Orangemen's views and felt that a service under their banner would cause widespread misapprehension.

Not surprisingly, pockets of prejudice among the clergy and

laiety of the area linger on, but when the cathedrals speak jointly, from the strength of balance between their followings, such prejudices can be swept under the carpet. Thus, at the time of the Metropolitan Cathedral's consecration, Edward Patey was well able to say: 'Nobody pretends that there are no great differences between us. But the old, unhappy story of enmity is more and more a thing of the past.

'Those who on the Anglican side fear that this new spirit of co-operation will "undo the work of the Reformation" fail to see that there is a new and greater reformation which is profoundly stirring all Christendom. In this renewal of our church life, Roman Catholics and Anglicans share alike.

'Half a century ago, two cathedrals in such close proximity would have been interpreted in terms of ecclesiastical rivalry. Today, at both ends of Hope Street, we rejoice at the new ecumenical spirit which has rightly been described as the great new fact of our era.'

At his morning service on the day of consecration, the Dean said that no city in Christendom afforded so great an opportunity for exploring the spirit of unity: 'Our relationship with the Roman Catholic Church still presents many difficult problems. We wish that they would accept Anglican Orders. We dislike their regulations about mixed marriages which we still find intolerable. We long to see religious tolerance practised in every country in the world in the spirit of the Vatican declaration on religious liberty. And we know that there are many Roman Catholics who fully share our view on these things.'

So what has been achieved? The cathedrals have exchanged preachers for certain services; they have alternated venues for annual non-denominational services such as those for the Red Cross, St John's Ambulance, and the regional hospitals (formerly held at Liverpool Cathedral every year); and there have also been joint staff meetings.

Beyond the cathedral precincts, the Roman Catholic Pastoral Council (the archdiocese's equivalent of the York Synod for the Anglican Northern Province) has included representatives of other denominations. The Church of

England representative is the cathedral's Canon Treasurer, Leslie Hopkins. The Anglican, Roman Catholic, and Free Churches also pay the salary of a full-time officer for the Merseyside Ecumenical Council, of which Dean Patey is chairman.

One year the Dean and Mgr Thomas McKenna, the first administrator at the Metropolitan Cathedral, took a joint party to the Holy Land. By this time Patey and McKenna were personal friends: Patey, who had previously been at Coventry, was regarded as something of an expert on the opening of new cathedrals, and he gave much advice to the Roman Catholics as they encountered teething troubles in the months leading up to the consecration.

But the major differences of dogma and officialdom still divide on basic issues. In this respect, the Roman Catholics are more hidebound than other denominations. Key stumbling points in Liverpool and elsewhere are centred on issues such as the infallibility of the Pope, and the doctrines and attitudes relating to the Virgin Mary.

Although the Second Vatican Council did much to thaw hitherto icy relationships—for instance, it admitted that all baptized belonged to Christ and could be regarded as 'separated brethren'—Roman Catholics are still not allowed to receive Communion outside their own Church, nor are their priests allowed to concelebrate with others.

While this is the official line—and there are plenty of examples in Liverpool of laymen breaking the rules by inter-Communion—it prevents the ecumenical exercise progressing at anything like the pace some would favour. Whereas clergy at the cathedral see the shared Eucharist as a step towards unity, the Roman Catholics view it as the ultimate act of any unity. 'It's rather like living in separate rooms and occasionally meeting on the landing,' says Canon Precentor Gordon Bates.

The cathedral views its real advance with the Metropolitan Cathedral hierarchy as dating from the friendship forged between Bishop Stuart Blanch and Archbishop Andrew Beck during the late 1960s. In fact, Beck's first attendance at a non-Roman Catholic Eucharist was the last one officiated at by Blanch before he became Archbishop of York. Beck came as a friend and observer. Although he was outwardly regarded as a conservative, his relationship with the Anglicans, enhanced by the Second Vatican Council, was far deeper than it had been under Heenan, who gave great verbal backing to the idea. The job of carrying on that friendship has now passed to Bishop David Sheppard and Archbishop Derek Worlock.

But there is a further complication, resulting from the way the cathedrals are run: the Dean and Chapter are in sole charge of Liverpool Cathedral. Dean Patey even offers the lighthearted remark that, having admitted a bishop to the building for enthronement, the first thing that happens 'is for us to put him in his place'. At the Metropolitan Cathedral, the administrator and clergy are curates directly responsible to the Archbishop. All that happens is subject to his personal approval. As a result, the activities at the 'Met' tend to be more strictly in line with formal liturgical usage. Nothing like the same amount of experimentation in worship has been carried out there.

The word ecumenism no longer attracts the attention of the media in the way it did twenty years ago. This is because there are limits which cannot be exceeded, while the ground which is firmly established is no longer newsworthy. However, the cathedral Chapter believe that real progress can still be made in the fields of education, social service, and overseas aid.

The Queen's Jubilee celebrations brought an overt demonstration of intent with a service shared between the two cathedrals. Its theme was thanksgiving and a joint pastoral letter from all of Merseyside's church leaders, issued to coincide with the event, began: 'Dear brothers and sisters in Jesus Christ', and went on to spell out the need for joint prayer and involvement in community affairs. When arrangements for the service were announced, another joint statement commented: 'Liverpool is a city which has seen religious antagonism. One of the salient features of the Liverpool scene in the reign of Queen Elizabeth II has been the almost complete elimination of this bitterness, to be replaced by a degree of ecumenical co-operation and friendship unique in the Queen's realm.'

Yet this service was symptomatic of the fact that the greatest examples of ecumenism arise when the acts of worship are urged upon the cathedrals by national or civic authorities. Apart from the weeks of prayer for Christian unity, and the odd 'special' occasion, no way has yet been found of establishing regular joint worship between the congregations of both buildings. Some feel that this is particularly disappointing in view of mutually thinning congregations for day-to-day services.

The two administrations do not so much work together, as work in qualified sympathy on different levels. However, the Anglican Church already has such differentials within its own ranks between High and Low churches, each serving the needs of individuals who wish to express their churchmanship in a particular way. But if at some future date ecumenism can be made to work on a large scale anywhere in Britain, Liverpool will surely provide a lead.

The potential is spread through all aspects of the cathedral's ministry, and extends to its music as well as its words and deeds. The choirs and organists have already made exchange visits for concerts and recitals, and when the Metropolitan Cathedral was opened, Patey and his Chapter commissioned an organ work, *Invocations*, by the Welsh composer William Mathias. This was then performed by Noel Rawsthorne, to whom it was dedicated, at the inaugural series of recitals.

The spirit of friendship which has stemmed from those years is now obvious in workaday contact. 'The whole feeling you have of being with other denominations is so different from what it was in the past,' says Chancellor Basil Naylor. 'The joint service for the Queen's Jubilee seemed perfectly natural to us. It would have been alarming ten years before. People would have wondered what had happened. The new cathedral coming into existence made a lot of difference. Certainly in Dean Dillistone's day, there was great friendship between the cathedral and other denominations. We would have been glad to have the Roman Catholics in, but there was a barrier before the Second Vatican Council. Now we feel that we know them over there.'

Today, clergy at both cathedrals will tell you that their buildings are complementary. They will also tell you that the 'Hope Street' talk is still mainly talk, and still at the courtesy stage. The Anglicans maintain that in the city of the Orange and the Green, both cathedrals had to be built. But those like Gordon Bates will add that 'if both were started again from scratch, it would be almost blasphemous and a denial of the way in which the Spirit has started to lead towards ecumenism.'

Perhaps even the architects would agree in the world of the 1970s and 1980s: Scott, the Roman Catholic, creating an Anglican edifice; Gibberd, the Free Churchman, designing a Roman Catholic church. So far, ecumenism has not been the most spectacular area of Liverpool Cathedral's work, but it promises to be one of the most exciting in the future.

Postscript

> Some day, perhaps it will be possible to study the art
> of public worship here, as music, or poetry, or drama
> are studied.
>
> CHARLES RAVEN

I once heard a rather pernicious joke that Liverpool Cathedral existed to cater for 'gay, black divorcees with rent arrears who wanted to join the Ecumenical Movement'. One could see the funny side of the remark, for by kaleidoscoping all those facets of circumstance together, the author (or authors) had followed the cardinal rule of humour, which is to exaggerate reality. But in telling the joke they had unearthed a profound truth: Liverpool Cathedral CARES for people—especially those whom the rest of society tends to shun and ignore. It is on the side of minorities who are discriminated against for political, moral, social, or economic reasons. And it is opposed to prejudice in any form.

Over the years the Chapter has backed the establishment and boxed it around the ears with equal resolve. When it has not approved of actions in High Church or high society, it has brought them low. For the biggest thing within the walls of this cathedral of cathedrals is a conscience which exerts a fearless opposition to those things which offend it.

The regular visitor or worshipper will gradually amass his own catalogue of personal experiences, both lighthearted and serious. I first came here with my father to hear the organ. I can still remember every detail of that initial conversation with Noel Rawsthorne, and that first glimpse of the monster console in the Central Space. As a newspaper critic, I still come to most of the recitals. But what has been added to that foundation of a love for music is a very high regard for the friendship and what has rightly been called the 'God-relatedness' of the cathedral's artistic and spiritual activity.

The late Poet Laureate, John Masefield, once summed up

129

17 Noel Rawsthorne at the great organ—the biggest Mersey Sound of them all.

his own feelings about cathedrals, at a luncheon to honour Giles Scott during the war: 'Besides being visible at a distance, a cathedral should be splendid within, with the best of all that artists and citizens can offer. This splendour should touch and mark all her parts and precincts, and not only her building, but all the many institutions attached to her, for teaching, healing, and relieving. She should be the place to which all the generosities of her citizens, as well as those of the artists of her time, should turn and flow.'

Masefield's ideas have certainly been realized. But what does fate ultimately have in store for Liverpool Cathedral? Here we have the mightiest of the 35,000 churches and chapels of various denominations in England alone. During the next five years 350 more churches will be declared redundant, to add to the list of more than 600 which closed between 1969 and 1977. Many of these churches will be turned into private homes (you can pick up a deconsecrated rural church for as

18 'All is safely gathered in . . .' A Harvest Festival service.

little as £500), shops, museums, youth hostels, restaurants, and bingo halls. Others will be demolished or preserved as monuments.

Heaven forbid that Liverpool Cathedral should ever become a museum. However, with inflation, the future may dictate that the building be run by a full-time financial administrator as well as a dean. It may also dictate that some form of government subsidy be introduced for maintenance, or that admission charges be made to visitors. Only time will tell. Whatever the outcome, its spiritual outreach, if maintained, will never be found wanting. My only suggestion, as an outside observer, would be to build up a counselling presence at the cathedral itself, for those who seek personal advice and guidance.

Canon Charles Raven once expressed the hope that 'some day, perhaps it will be possible to study the art of public worship here, as music, or poetry, or drama, are studied'. I hope that the preceding pages have gone some way towards fulfilling that wish. Yet it would not have been possible to write this book without help from so many different people. I must thank in particular Dean Edward Patey, his Chapter and staff, for allowing me to base myself at the cathedral for two months in order to undertake the work, and for giving me valuable advice and co-operation.

Perhaps I may be forgiven the indulgence of signing off with some favourite lines by William Wordsworth. They have a timeless quality which makes them most applicable to Liverpool Cathedral:

> Give all thou canst; high Heaven rejects the lore
> Of nicely-calculated less or more;
> So deemed the man who fashioned for the sense
> These lofty pillars, spread that branching roof
> Self-poised, and scooped into ten thousand cells,
> Where light and shade repose, where music dwells
> Lingering – and wandering on as loth to die;
> Like thoughts whose very sweetness yieldeth proof
> That they were born for immortality.

APPENDICES

Appendices

SOME USEFUL FACTS AT A GLANCE

Liverpool Cathedral is the fifth largest cathedral in the world. This is calculated by the area of the building interior. Liverpool comprises 104,275 sq ft, compared with St Peter's, Rome (227,069 sq ft); Seville Cathedral (132,120 sq ft); Milan Cathedral (125,865 sq ft); and St John the Divine, New York (121,000 sq ft).

It has the highest vaulting in the world—175 ft max at Undertower.

It is the second longest cathedral in the world, at 619 ft.

The tower contains the highest and heaviest ringing peal of bells in the world—at 219 ft above floor level.

The tower is supported by the highest Gothic arches ever built—107 ft at apices.

The tower is 331 ft high—347 ft above St James's Road.

The Choir vault is 116 ft high.

The Nave vault is 120 ft high.

BISHOPS OF LIVERPOOL

1880–1900 John Charles Ryle, *b.* 1816, *d.* 1900
1900–1923 Francis James Chavasse, *b.* 1846, *d.* 1928
1923–1944 Albert Augustus David, *b.* 1867, *d.* 1950
1944–1965 Clifford Arthur Martin, *b.* 1895, *d.* 1977
1965–1974 Stuart Yarworth Blanch, *b.* 1918
1975–   David Sheppard, *b.* 1929

THE CATHEDRAL CHAPTER

Members in November 1977

Dean	The Very Revd E. H. Patey
Residentiary Canons	The Revd C. B. Naylor, Chancellor
	The Revd L. E. Hopkins, Treasurer
	The Revd G. E. Bates, Precentor
	The Ven C. E. Corbett, Archdeacon

THE HISTORY OF THE CHAPTER

1910 On the consecration of the Lady Chapel as the Cathedral of the Diocese the Bishop of Liverpool, DR F. J. CHAVASSE, became, under the Cathedral Act of 1902, the Acting Dean, and he appointed—

> CANON H. E. BILBROUGH, then Rector of Liverpool and later Bishop of Newcastle, as Sub-Dean.

1916 THE VENERABLE ARCHDEACON SPOONER succeeded Canon Bilbrough as Sub-Dean on the latter's appointment as Bishop of Dover.

1923 An Endowment Fund having been provided, Bishop Chavasse appointed the VENERABLE ARCHDEACON HOWSON, and the REVD MORLEY STEVENSON, as Provisional Canons.

1923 DR DAVID, third Bishop of Liverpool, succeeded Dr Chavasse as acting Dean.

1924 The Bishop of Liverpool appointed the following to be additional members of the Provisional Chapter—

> THE REVD W. THOMPSON ELLIOTT (Provisional Canon and Sub-Dean);
>
> THE VENERABLE ARCHDEACON G. H. SPOONER (Provisional Canon and Chancellor);
>
> THE REVD CHARLES E. RAVEN (Provisional Canon).

1925 THE REVD F. W. DWELLY appointed a Provisional Canon.

1926 THE REVD F. W. HEAD appointed a Provisional Canon and Sub-Dean in succession to Canon Thompson Elliott, who resigned on his appointment as Vicar of Leeds.

1929 CANON F. W. HEAD resigned on his appointment as Archbishop of Melbourne.

> CANON F. W. DWELLY appointed Vice-Dean.

1930 CANON MORLEY STEVENSON died.

1931 In accordance with Liverpool Cathedral Act 1885, an order in Council was issued establishing a permanent Dean and four Residentiary Canons to be the Principal Chapter of the Cathedral, the Dean being appointed by the Crown and the Canons by the Bishop. The following were appointed—

Dean: THE VERY REVD F. W. DWELLY

Residentiary Canons:

> THE REVD C. E. RAVEN (Chancellor);
> THE REVD T. E. A. DAVEY
> THE REVD J. C. HOW (part-time)
> THE REVD C. F. TWITCHETT (part-time)

1932   THE REVD J. S. BEZZANT appointed to succeed Canon Raven who resigned on his appointment as Regius Professor of Divinity at Cambridge.

1933   CANON J. T. MITCHELL appointed Canon Residentiary part-time in place of Canon Twitchett who resigned on his appointment as Archdeacon of Warrington.

1935   THE RT REVD H. GRESFORD JONES, Bishop of Warrington, appointed Canon Residentiary in place of Canon How who resigned on his appointment as Vicar of Brighton.

1938   CANON W. E. H. MORRIS appointed Canon Residentiary (part-time) in place of Canon Mitchell who retired.

1944   CANON DAVEY died.
        CANON C. F. H. SOULBY appointed Canon Residentiary (part-time).

1952   CANON SOULBY died.
        CANON BEZZANT retired on his appointment as Dean of St John's College, Cambridge.
        THE REVD F. W. DILLISTONE appointed Canon Residentiary and Chancellor in place of Canon Bezzant.

1955   THE VERY REVD F. W. DWELLY, Dean of Liverpool, retired.
        BISHOP GRESFORD JONES retired.
        CANON F. H. PERKINS appointed Canon Residentiary (part-time) in place of Canon Soulby.

1956   CANON F. W. DILLISTONE appointed Dean of Liverpool.
        CANON C. B. NAYLOR appointed Canon Residentiary and Chancellor in place of Canon Dillistone.
        THE REVD R. NELSON appointed Canon Residentiary (part-time) in place of Bishop Gresford Jones.
        CANON MORRIS retired.

1957   CANON NELSON resigned on appointment as Bishop of Middleton.

1958   CANON R. B. PARKER appointed Canon Residentiary (part-time) in place of Canon Nelson.

1960   CANON F. A. REDWOOD appointed Canon Residentiary (part-time) in place of Canon Morris.

1961   CANON PARKER resigned on his appointment to Wellington College.

1962   THE REVD H. ELLIS appointed Canon Residentiary (part-time) in place of Canon Parker, and Canon Precentor.

1963   DEAN DILLISTONE resigned.

1964   CANON E. H. PATEY appointed Dean.

CANON C. E. RAVEN died.

CANON F. A. REDWOOD died shortly after retiring.

WALTER HENRY GOSS-CUSTARD died.

REVD L. F. HOPKINS appointed Canon Residentiary (part-time) in place of Canon F. H. Perkins who retired.

REVD E. HICKSON (Diocesan Canon) appointed Guest-Master in succession to Canon Redwood.

1967   CANON J. S. BEZZANT died.

1968   THE VENERABLE ARCHDEACON WILKINSON appointed Canon Residentiary (part-time).

REVD J. P. THORNTON-DUESBERY appointed Canon Theologian.

CANON H. MORRIS died.

1969   DEACONESS TOMLINSON appointed Cathedral Chaplain.

1970   ARCHDEACON WILKINSON retired as Canon Residentiary and Archdeacon of Liverpool.

1971   REVD C. E. CORBETT appointed Archdeacon of Liverpool and Canon Residentiary.

REVD DAVID STEVENS appointed Honorary Canon.

1972   CANON HENRY ELLIS died.

REVD W. E. A. LOCKETT appointed Canon Theologian.

1973   REVD G. E. BATES appointed Precentor and Canon Residentiary.

REVD D. HESKETH appointed Honorary Canon.

1975   CANON HICKSON died, succeeded by CANON L. F. HOPKINS as Guest-Master.

1977   CANON DAVID STEVENS left the Diocese to join the Franciscan Community in Dorset.

Organist:

NOEL RAWSTHORNE who succeeded H. GOSS-CUSTARD who retired in 1955.

Choirmaster:

RONALD WOAN who succeeded E. C. ROBINSON who retired in 1948.

BUILDERS AND WORKMEN

Foremen

F. Bricknell

A. Coventry

F. Daniels

C. Hannaway

T. Rowbottom

H. Thomas

Workmen associated with the building for many years.

T. Begley (Labourer)
J. Birchall (Slinger)
S. Birchall (Cranedriver)
A. Boothroyd (Mason)
W. Brophy (Mason)
G. Burdett (Mason)
G. J. Burdett (Mason)
C. Burns (Mason)
F. Butler (Slinger)
E. Casey (Scaffolder)
T. Clarke (Cranedriver)
C. Cowley (Machinist)
G. Cooke (Cranedriver)
A. Crickson (Mason)
E. Davidson (Labourer)
H. Davies (Mason)
J. Drapala (Cranedriver)
P. Dunn (Mason)
E. Filson (Mason)
P. Flinn (Mason)
T. Gibbons (Cranedriver)
G. Griffiths (Mason)
C. Grimes (Cranedriver)
J. Hewitt (Slinger)
J. H. Hewitt (Cranedriver)
J. Hilton (Clerk)
J. Hodgin (Cranedriver)
D. Holland (Mason)
C. Holloway (Mason)
C. Hughes (Scaffolder Mate)
E. Ireland (Fitter)

J. Ireland (Mason)
A. Johnson (Mason)
S. Jones (Sawyer)
C. Kaye (Quarryman)
J. Ker (Scaffolder)
R. Lund (Sawyer)
E. Malone (Quarryman)
E. Mason (Simplex)
G. Mason (Mason)
J. McDermott (Mason)
L. McDonald (Mason)
J. Nye (Quarryman)
R. Parr (Mason)
C. Ramsey (Mason)
K. Redman (Mason)
R. Revill (Quarryman)
J. Rowson (Labourer)
R. Royds (Plumber)
F. Rudkin (Sawyer)
E. Seal (Mason)
R. Shaw (Blacksmith)
A. Smith (Mason)
J. Smith (Bricklayer)
H. Southern (Quarryman)
C. Swinnerton (Slinger)
N. Todd (Mason)
J. Walker (Mason)
J. Whitehill (Mason)
C. Williams (Mason)
D. Williams (Machinist)
J. L. Worrall (Mason)

The author is grateful for permission to use part of the appendices from Vere Cotton's *Book of Liverpool Cathedral* (now out of print); and to Miss Patience Thompson for updating the information.